ST. DY… 'S PL… BOOK

"If you experience mental health symptoms or love someone who does, you will find Tommy Tighe's book moving and helpful. He provides hopeful, practical tools to utilize immediately and blends wisdom from saints, scripture, and clinical experience into the perfect mix of relatability and sound psychological advice. I will be recommending *St. Dymphna's Playbook* to many people."

Regina Boyd

Catholic mental health professional and host of the podcast *Connecting Out Loud*

"Very few people can speak with authority about the interplay between traditional mental health treatment and the healing power of the divine, but Tommy Tighe does so in *St. Dymphna's Playbook* with compassion, vulnerability, and wisdom. If, like me, you have ever struggled with depression, anxiety, or any other mental health disorder, this is the guide for which you've been waiting. This beautiful gift of a book will transform a great many lives."

Hallie Lord

Author of *Falling Home*

"Whether you struggle with mental health or support someone who does, *St. Dymphna's Playbook* is an essential read that illuminates common experiences around depression, anxiety, trauma, relationships, and grief. It's accessible, easy to comprehend, and a great gift to our Church, full of practical tools and abundant in hope."

Scott Weeman

Founder and executive director of Catholic in Recovery

"There are valuable insights in *St. Dymphna's Playbook* to help Catholic leaders minister to people living with mental health challenges and illnesses. In addition to professional guidance, this book also shows how the saints—many of whom lived with mental illnesses themselves—can guide you in your ministry."

Deacon Ed Shoener

President of the Association of Catholic Mental Health Ministers
Compiler and editor of *Responding to Suicide: A Pastoral Handbook for Catholic Leaders*

ST. DYMPHNA'S PLAYBOOK

A CATHOLIC GUIDE TO FINDING MENTAL AND EMOTIONAL WELL-BEING

TOMMY TIGHE

Ave Maria Press AVE Notre Dame, Indiana

Founded in 1865, Ave Maria Press is a ministry of the United States Province of Holy Cross.

www.avemariapress.com

Paperback: ISBN-13 978-1-64680-088-9

E-book: ISBN-13 978-1-64680-089-6

Cover image © Barbulat / iStock / Getty Images Plus.

Cover and text design by Sam Watson.

Printed and bound in the United States of America.

Library of Congress Cataloging-in-Publication Data is available.

To Karen, James, Paul, Andy, Luke, and Charlie.
You have helped me grow in ways I never
could have believed possible. You are all God's
greatest blessing in my life.

CONTENTS

Relationships

Grief

INTRODUCTION

LORD, THE ONE YOU LOVE IS SICK

"Come to me, all you who labor and are burdened, and I will give you rest. Take my yoke upon you and learn from me, for I am meek and humble of heart; and you will find rest for yourselves. For my yoke is easy, and my burden light" (Mt 11:28–30). I frequently call to mind these words of Jesus to bring me peace amid the emotional turmoil and mental health struggles of my daily life. Jesus Christ is the answer to every question we find ourselves asking out of the depths of our hearts. But what does that mean? Recognizing the power of a relationship with Christ in our lives, the sufficiency of his grace for all our needs, and the strength and hope found in his Passion, Death, and Resurrection is an incredible first step. But too often we hear or acknowledge that he is the answer and then try to figure out what comes next on our own.

In our own life experience, we can see how there must be another step after accepting faith that Jesus wants us to take to find healing and peace. We feel paralyzed with anxiety and pray for relief but find none. We feel bedridden with depression and cry out to God for help, but we see no results. We become terrorized by our past traumas and beg for peace from above, but we still find ourselves plagued. We feel left with contemplating other deep, painful questions: *Why would God allow these symptoms into my life? Is God not healing me because I'm not praying hard enough or believing in him enough? Why would an all-loving God permit this kind of suffering for me?*

In Christian circles we often hear, "God loves you exactly as you are, but he loves you too much to leave you that way." I've contemplated this phrase and how it applies to our journey toward mental wellness.

St. Paul famously says in Romans 8:28, "We know that all things work for good for those who love God, who are called according to his purpose," and that line, too, is quickly tossed in the general direction of those who are suffering. While God may bring something good out of our suffering, that distant good isn't the entire story. God loves us too much to allow us to stay in those things that bring us pain, doubt, and suffering and that inhibit our ability to experience his peace.

As we go through this book, we do so while contemplating different words from St. Paul, where he gives us a lifeline of hope, a connection to the loving God we all seek when we're traveling through the darkness: "First of all, then, I ask that supplications, prayers, petitions, and thanksgivings be offered for everyone . . . that we may lead a quiet and tranquil life in all devotion and dignity. This is good and pleasing to God our savior, who wills everyone to be saved and to come to knowledge of the truth" (1 Tm 2:1–4).

God wills that everyone be saved, not just from sin and evil but also from depression, anxiety, past trauma, difficult relationships, heartbreak, addiction, and everything else that brings us pain, suffering, and separation from the love and peace God so desperately wants to give us.

First, we must come to the knowledge of that truth.

Then we have to live it and learn to see where in our lives God's saving peace is waiting to heal us.

Let's go on the journey together.

My name is Tommy. I'm a mental health professional, a husband, and a father of five boys, and I'm here to fill the void of Catholic conversations about mental health. I graduated with a master of arts in clinical psychology in 2005, and after collecting more than three thousand hours of clinical training, I became a licensed marriage and family therapist in 2009 and since then have been working closely with individuals and their family members as they experience the ups and downs of persistent mental health symptoms.

Most importantly, I've lived with mental health symptoms myself, and I've learned that one key to living with these symptoms is being open about them and their causes. I've experienced grief to the point of praying God would take my life. I've walked through anxiety and fear that have led to panic attacks. I've heard God's call to bring compassion and comfort to those who are trying their best with the suffering life brings, and I pray that he will give all of us the grace to answer that call for ourselves and all our sisters and brothers.

Lord, the One You Love Is Sick

In the Gospel of John, we encounter a story about Jesus that helps us feel the depths of his humanity like few others:

> Now a man was ill, Lazarus from Bethany, the village of Mary and her sister Martha. Mary was the one who had anointed the Lord with perfumed oil and dried his feet with her hair; it was her brother Lazarus who was ill. So the sisters sent word to him, saying, "*Master, the one you love is ill. . . .*" Now Jesus loved Martha and her sister and Lazarus. So when he heard that he was ill, he remained for two days in the place where he was. Then after this he said to his disciples, "Let us go back to Judea. . . ."
>
> When Jesus arrived, he found that Lazarus had already been in the tomb for four days. . . . When Martha heard that Jesus was coming, she went to meet him; but Mary sat at home. Martha said to Jesus, "*Lord, if you had been here, my brother would not have died.* [But] even now I know that whatever you ask of God, God will give you." Jesus said to her, "Your brother will rise. . . ."
>
> When Jesus saw her weeping and the Jews who had come with her weeping, he became perturbed and deeply troubled, and said, "Where have you laid him?" They said to him, "Sir, come and see." *And Jesus wept. . . .*
>
> And Jesus raised his eyes and said, "Father, I thank you for hearing me. I know that you always hear me; but because of the crowd here I have said this, that they may believe that you sent me." And when he had said this, he cried out in a loud voice, "Lazarus, come out!" The dead man came out, tied hand and foot with burial bands, and his face was wrapped in a cloth. So Jesus said to them, "Untie him and let him go." (Jn 11:1–3, 5–7, 17, 20–23, 33–35, 41–44; emphasis added)

There are three lines from that story that I go back to again and again, especially in times of suffering.

Master, the one you love is ill. The words of the sisters of Lazarus constitute the simplest prayer I can think of when we or someone we love is suffering. It reminds me of the words of the Blessed Virgin Mary at the wedding feast at Cana: "They have no wine" (Jn 2:3). These statements, these intercessions made to Jesus by those he loved, provide us with a blueprint for how we should be reaching out to him in our time of need. There's no need for poetic language; there's no need for long explanations; in fact, there's no need even for asking for a specific solution. Jesus knows what we need before we ask, before the thought is even in our minds, and he knows—far better than we could even imagine—what would be best for us in any given situation.

Lord, if you had been here, my brother would not have died. This statement became a prayer of sorts for me during our greatest trial, the death of our son. The words of Lazarus's sister are ones that we all use at certain points in our lives, when suffering and darkness descend on us and we're left wondering where God can be found in it all. We're told that all we need to do is ask and it will be given to us. And while that's most certainly true, we often misunderstand it to mean that everything will work out the way we want it to, which is most certainly not the case, and we're left calling out to Jesus, "Lord, if you had been here, my brother would not have died."

Jesus responds to us, just as he did in the gospel story, by reminding us that everything "is for the glory of God, that the Son of God may be glorified through it" (Jn 11:4). It's hard for us to hear and to incorporate into our hearts, but everything that happens to us is meant for the glory of God. That doesn't always make things easier, though, which is why I always come back to *And Jesus wept.*

Didn't Jesus know that he was going to raise his friend Lazarus from the dead? Of course. Didn't Jesus realize that pain and suffering here in this world is nothing compared to the glory awaiting us on the other side? Undoubtedly, he did. And yet he *still* wept over the death of his friend? Assuredly.

Even though Jesus has defeated death, even though Jesus presents to all of us an eternal life that will make up for all our pain and anguish, he still understands the sorrow and weeps with us. There is no claim in the Christian faith that because we have faith we won't experience the sorrow associated with suffering. Quite the opposite. Instead, the Christian faith claims that Christ weeps and suffers with us, and that brings us comfort.

How to Use This Book

This is *not* meant to be a self-help book.

While there are coping skills within this book for the various mental health experiences we may be going through, this book doesn't intend to solve all our problems. It's meant to remind us that we are not alone. Others are suffering just like us. My hope is that this book provides the impetus for *our* Catholic Church to bring our mental health struggles out into the open *without* stigma and *with* a plan for moving forward.

Each chapter in the book is dedicated to a different mental health experience we may be going through. In the case of the section on relationships, those experiences are not strictly a mental health experience, but they are emotions and experiences that can negatively affect our mental health, and they deserve to be discussed. Each contains a reflection; an explanation of what the symptoms or diagnosis actually is; practical, healthy coping skills we can all try; a brief exploration of what our faith and the saints have to say about the experience; and a list of key points we can all look to when the idea of reading an entire chapter seems overwhelming.

This book is less about having an answer for everything and more about trying to foster a Catholic community where we all suffer together, unafraid to walk forward with our sisters and brothers through their valley of tears. With that in mind, if you find yourself in a situation where you recognize you need more help than this book can provide, please flip to the "Resources" section in the back and reach out to the ones that most fit your needs. You are never alone. Help and hope are always out there.

As Servant of God Dorothy Day once wrote, "We have all known the long loneliness and we have learned that the only solution is love and that love comes with community."[1] If this book paves the way for the growth of community for those of us Catholics struggling with our mental health, it will have accomplished more than I ever could have dreamed.

Why St. Dymphna?

Many times I have been asked various questions about St. Dymphna, the patron saint of those suffering from mental illness and those who care for them. Why is *she* the patron of mental health when it seems as though she was simply the victim of a homicidal mentally ill father? How did she become associated with interceding for those suffering from mental illness? How in the world do you pronounce her name?!

Dymphna was born in seventh-century Ireland, the daughter of a Christian mother and a pagan father named Damon who reigned over Oriel, a small kingdom on the north side of the island. Dymphna was just fourteen years old when her mother became sick and died. Dymphna had recently taken a vow of chastity, dedicating her life to Christ, thanks to her mother's witness to the faith.

After her mother's death, Dymphna's father began to spiral into grief and bereavement, to the point where her father's friends recommended he get remarried as a way to move forward. He agreed, but he vowed only to marry someone who had the beauty of his decreased wife. His friends scoured the land nearby to find a woman of matching beauty, but they came up empty, which led Dymphna's father to fall deeper into grief and eventually into a madness that focused his desires on Dymphna. He was unceasing in his efforts to convince her to marry him, but she pushed back and eventually escaped with her spiritual director to Geel, Belgium. It was there that she gained the reputation of compassion and kindness that would directly lead to her becoming the patron saint for those suffering from mental illness.

An article from fellow Dymphna fan Anne Thériault shares what happened next:

> Dymphna . . . use[d] her considerable resources to build a hospice for the poor and sick. According to some versions of her legend, this hospice particularly served those with mental or neurological illnesses. If this is true, Dymphna would have been centuries ahead of the rest of Europe. Most medieval hospices turned away people with mental illness, believing them to be contagious or possessed or both. But Dymphna seemed determined to help others who suffered the way her father did.[2]

Dymphna's compassion and charity would eventually be her undoing, however, as her father's friends eventually discovered her whereabouts and her father, ever-deepening into his madness, tracked her down:

> After finding her, Damon had her priest executed in front of her. But even that didn't convince Dymphna to marry him, so Damon beheaded her with his own sword. . . .
>
> Some traditions hold that mentally ill patients from her hospice also witnessed Dymphna's death, and they were immediately, miraculously cured. As this story spread, Geel became a place of pilgrimage for the "mad"—anyone with mental illness, epilepsy, neurological disorders and cognitive differences. Pilgrims flocked to Dymphna's burial site, and more cures were recorded. At some point, she began to be venerated as a local saint.[3]

With all that, two of the questions I've frequently been asked about this heroic saint have been answered.

The pronunciation of her name, on the other hand? Well, I'll just keep trying my best . . .

DEPRESSION

1. ANHEDONIA

LORD, THE ONE YOU LOVE FEELS NOTHING

Sitting on the couch, blankly starting ahead, the noise of three young children playing right in front of me in the living room became nothing more than background static. Our oldest walked up to me to ask if he could play video games. I just nodded, unable to speak, or rather not really caring enough to say anything in reply. Our youngest spilled a package of crackers on the entryway floor, and I just cleaned it up. No words were said. No emotion was felt.

This was a daily routine in our home in the days and weeks following the death of our newborn in the spring of 2016. Sure, there were tears, anger, a feeling of hopelessness. But above everything else, there was *nothing*.

I felt numb.

When most of us think of depression, we tend to think of uncontrollable sobbing, persistent negative thinking about ourselves and our situation, and still more uncontrollable sobbing. While those are certainly painful symptoms to deal with, perhaps the most troubling effects of depression in our lives are apathy and anhedonia.

Sitting on that couch all those years ago, overcome by a complete lack of feeling, I was living in a moment where I didn't care about anything and I was completely unable to experience any kind of joy or pleasure. When we're depressed, it's precisely this lack of feeling that brings us to our knees. In feeling heartbreak, balling our eyes out, and experiencing the searing pain of depression, we're at least feeling *something*. When we're in that place where we feel nothing and nothing brings us even a hint of pleasure, we're lost, we're desperate, and we need help.

Depression Isn't Just Feeling Sad

We often use the term *depressed* interchangeably with the experience of feeling sad, which has led our culture as a whole to see depression as much less serious than it is. Also, it has reinforced the idea that people should be able to just "get over" their depression because "Look at me! I was sad earlier this week and I just decided to feel better!"

It's vital for us to understand exactly what the word *depression* means. According to the *Diagnostic and Statistical Manual of Mental Disorders*, the guidebook of the mental health profession, to be diagnosed with major depressive disorder requires at least five symptoms to be present in a two-week period. These symptoms include depressed mood, diminished interest or loss of pleasure in almost all activities (anhedonia), significant weight change, recurrent thoughts of death, and more.[1] In this chapter, we're specifically looking at anhedonia, the inability to feel or even be interested in pleasure.

It can sound minor at face value, but if you really stop to think about all the brief and seemingly insignificant moments of pleasure you have throughout your days, you can start to understand how awful you would feel if those moments and experiences were snatched away. On the website Psych Central, Margarita Tartakovsky conveyed one author's description of his anhedonia: "I couldn't laugh, I couldn't cry, I couldn't think clearly. My head was in a black cloud and nothing in the outside world had any impact. The only relief that came was through sleep, and my biggest dread was waking up knowing that I had to get through another 15 hours before I could sleep again."[2]

So What Do We Do?

Depression attacks our concentration, focus, and motivation, so we're quite literally impaired in our ability to come up with solutions when we're in the midst of it. So, first, don't be hard on yourself if you can't come up with healthy skills and actually do them on the fly! Instead, we write down *when we're feeling well* a list of healthy coping skills that work for us.

Next, realize that not every coping skill you hear or read about is going to help you. You have to find the skills that resonate with you, that speak to you, that you have tried and found to be helpful. I'm focusing here on those that help us directly cope with this distressing experience of anhedonia and the lack of feeling anything; however, they can also be helpful with other symptoms of depression.

Physical activity is an important coping skill. Obviously, we don't have much motivation to be physically active when we're feeling depressed, but even starting out small can have huge benefits to our mental health when we're stuck in this situation. We get an uptick in adrenaline in response to physical activity, which can be one physical way to combat what anhedonia is doing to us.

Prayer is another go-to coping skill for anhedonia. Depression can inhibit our ability to feel motivated to pray. However, as many Catholic spiritual giants can attest to, prayer when we feel unmotivated, unmoved, and uninterested can have huge spiritual benefits, as it helps us connect with God, put our experience into words, and sometimes focus on others instead of our own depression. Having a recurring prayer schedule that you engage in when you're feeling good can come in handy when you need that stability and quiet time for meditation when you're not feeling it.

Interacting with others is another coping skill that sounds impossible when we're mired in the dark hopelessness. Yet meaningful social interactions can be a savior when we're experiencing anhedonia. In fact, the effect on our brain from positive social interaction or physical touch from someone we care about can completely turn things around. According to the professionals at Tree House Recovery, "Physical connection with other humans like hugs, holding, or even intercourse produces the neurotransmitter oxytocin. Although it is frequently called the 'love hormone' oxytocin also decreases cortisol levels. And since high cortisol levels produce symptoms of depression and anhedonia, lowering cortisol levels will also decrease those symptoms."[3]

Is There Healing and Relief Out There?

There is always hope, even when our lives become so overwhelmingly dark that we can no longer see it. While coping skills can and will help, they also take time and practice. So we must practice our coping skills when we're feeling well. But how do we know when it's time to get help? How do we know when it's time to get started with talk therapy? How do we know when it's time for us to consider taking medication for our mental health symptoms?

These are hard questions to answer, *and* there are different answers for each person who asks them. We begin by assessing whether our mental health symptoms are impairing our ability to function:

- Are we still connecting with family and friends, or are we isolating more than before?
- Are we still getting up on time, getting to work, and focusing during our workday?
- Are we attending classes at school and getting our schoolwork done as before?
- Are we maintaining our housing, or is our mental health experience leading us to no longer care about making rent payments?
- Are we showering, brushing our teeth, and just generally taking care of ourselves like before?
- Are we still exercising, eating as well as we normally would, and taking all medications prescribed to us as they are prescribed?
- Are we noticing that we're using substances way more than before? Are we getting involved in risky behavior leading to interactions with the police?

When we start to answer yes to these questions, we know that it's time to reach out for help. Ideally we will reach out for help *just before* we start answering yes to these types of questions, but it can be really hard to recognize that we're heading in that direction until we see an objective reality that we can name.

All that being said, we should feel free to reach out for help and explore options for therapy or medication for our mental health *at any time*. We don't need to wait to reach a specific level of suffering. And exploring options in therapy or medication doesn't mean we're committed to doing so for the foreseeable future.

In fact, getting involved in therapy when we're well is healthy. It's helpful to have an outside perspective on our lives, one that isn't attached to us emotionally, to help give us a different way of looking at things. The same can be said of medication. If you feel as though you might need medication to help with your mental health experience, explore options with your doctor before you're in a crisis.

There *is* healing, hope, and opportunity for relief out there. If you're coping with anhedonia and mired in the inability to feel anything at all, please realize that you're not alone and you can feel again.

What the Bible Says about Anhedonia

> The enemy has pursued my soul;
>   he has crushed my life to the ground.
> He has made me dwell in darkness
>   like those long dead.
> My spirit is faint within me;
>   my heart despairs.
> I remember the days of old;
>   I ponder all your deeds;
>   the works of your hands I recall.
> I stretch out my hands toward you,
>   my soul to you like a parched land.
> Hasten to answer me, LORD;
>   for my spirit fails me.
> Do not hide your face from me,
>   lest I become like those descending to the pit.
>
> —Psalm 143:3–7

When it comes to depression, hopelessness, and anhedonia, we have a precious friend in the psalms. The psalms can help us find the words for prayer that can be difficult to formulate on our own when we're struggling with depression. They aren't afraid to convey the feelings we experience as human beings. They don't hold back in describing difficult feelings and in sharing those feelings directly with God. Sometimes we have this sense that we must hide from God the worst thoughts within us, pretending that he can't see right through us. The psalms provide the antidote to that idea, showing us that screaming out our suffering directly at God without holding anything back is precisely what he wants us to do. "Caged in, I cannot escape; my eyes grow dim from trouble. All day I call on you, LORD; I stretch out my hands to you. . . . I have been mortally afflicted since youth; I have borne your terrors and I am made numb" (Ps 88:9–10, 16; see also Psalm 88:4–19).

I am made numb. And yet the Bible also offers hope in the midst of this dark valley. Proverbs 3:5—"Trust in the LORD with all your heart, on your own intelligence do not rely"—helps us to realize that the darkness and hopelessness we see all around us is not the final word. We cannot rely solely on our experience and what we see happening before us. There is something deeper going on, something we can't experience with our senses. As St. Paul says, "We are afflicted in every way, but not constrained; perplexed, but not driven to despair; persecuted, but not abandoned; struck down, but not destroyed" (2 Cor 4:8–9).

We are not constrained, not driven to despair, not abandoned.

We are not destroyed.

But not because healing, comfort, and peace are waiting right around the corner. Not always. Our experience in life reminds us of that again and again. Rather, we have our eyes set on the future that awaits us because of God's promise: "He will wipe every tear from their eyes, and there shall be no more death or mourning, wailing or pain, [for] the old order has passed away" (Rv 21:4).

What the Saints Say about Anhedonia

> In my soul I feel just that terrible pain of loss . . . of God not wanting me—of God not being God—of God not existing . . . I find no words to express the depths of the darkness.
>
> —St. Teresa of Calcutta

Servant of God Dorothy Day once famously said, "Don't call me a saint. I don't want to be dismissed that easily."[4] At first glance, this may seem like an odd sentiment, but if we honestly look at our popular opinions of saints, we can start to see more clearly what Day meant.

It's all too easy to pack the saints into nice tidy boxes. St. Francis of Assisi? A man who lived a life of poverty and believed in taking care of nature. St. Maximilian Kolbe? A man who was willing to sacrifice his own life for the sake of another during one of history's most terrifying moments. St. Teresa of Calcutta? A woman who lived among the poorest of the poor, unafraid to find Christ in the darkest of circumstances. While all those descriptors are true, they also push away any ambiguity, any struggle, any hardship. And as Day hinted at, they dismiss the individuals far too easily.

It's precisely the complicated and conflicting parts of St. Teresa of Calcutta's journey that may have the most to offer us. Born in 1910 into a Kosovar Albanian family, Anjezë Gonxhe Bojaxhiu was baptized into the faith on the day after her birth and left home at eighteen to join the Sisters of Loreto in Ireland, with the goal of becoming a missionary.[5] In 1929, she began to teach at a school near her convent in Darjeeling, India. When she made her vows, she took on the name Teresa in honor of St. Thérèse of Lisieux. She took her final vows in 1937; however, on September 10, 1946, she experienced a very different call while riding on a train for her annual retreat that would send her life in a radically different way: "I was to leave the convent and help the poor while living among them. It was an order. To fail would have been to break the faith."[6]

With that, she embarked on her mission to become the woman we all know and love today, Mother Teresa, and eventually was canonized on September 4, 2016, by Pope Francis. It's the insights contained in her letters posthumously released, however, that have drawn me closer to her. In 1957, she wrote the following words to her spiritual director:

> In the darkness . . . Lord, my God, who am I that you should forsake me? The child of your love—and now become as the most hated one. The one—you have thrown away as unwanted—unloved. I call, I cling, I want, and there is no one to answer. . . . Where I try to raise my thoughts to heaven, there is such convicting emptiness that those very thoughts return like sharp knives and hurt my very soul. Love—the word—it brings nothing. I am told God lives in me—and

> yet the reality of darkness and coldness and emptiness is so great that nothing touches my soul.[7]

Even so, she pushed forward. She continued to live an incredible and inspiring life, all while having this spiritual anhedonia that so many of us have walked through in our own lives. If you've ever felt like me, sitting on the couch feeling absolutely nothing, wondering if you'll ever experience the joys and pleasures of life ever again, please remember that there is hope, healing, and a community out there ready and willing to walk with you through this dark night. And you may not have realized it until now, but St. Teresa of Calcutta is there for you too!

IN BRIEF

- Anhedonia, a common experience of depression, is the presence of a pervasive diminished interest or loss of pleasure in almost all activities.
- It's important to write down *when we're feeling well* a list of healthy coping skills that work for us, rather than waiting until we're struggling with our symptoms.
- Physical activity, prayer, and interacting with our social supports are coping skills, but we need to practice them *when we're feeling well* so we'll be prepared.
- With persistent anhedonia, many find therapy to be helpful, while others may also need medication to help them combat the situation.
- When it comes to depression, hopelessness, and anhedonia, we all have a precious friend in the psalms (for example, Psalms 39, 143, and 88).

CLOSING PRAYER

> O Christ Jesus, when all is darkness and we feel our weakness and helplessness, give us the sense of Your Presence, Your Love, and Your Strength. Help us to have perfect trust in Your protecting

love and strengthening power, so that nothing may frighten or worry us. For living close to You, we shall see Your Hand, Your Purpose, Your Will, through all things.

—St. Ignatius of Loyola

2. IRRITABILITY

LORD, THE ONE YOU LOVE IS ANNOYED WITH EVERYTHING

When we have a bad day, we can take the time to do a little self-introspection and realize that we might be more irritable than usual. Then we can do some things to help us turn our mood around: go for a walk, take some time to meditate, watch or read something that lightens our mood. The reason we're able to do this, even though we've had a hard day, is that our brain is still functioning at a level where we're able to recognize what's driving our reactions and behaviors and then have the energy and motivation to do something about it.

In the midst of depression, however, our brain is hampered in its ability to function. We're more tired than usual, less able to concentrate or tolerate frustration, and less motivated to do anything about it. Even the smallest of annoyances can cause intense irritability and anger.

Depression Limits Our Brain's Capacity

When we talk about depression, we almost always frame it as a deep and lasting sadness, loneliness, decreased motivation, decreased energy, and perhaps even suicidal thinking. When I was in grad school learning how to be a therapist, irritability was also typically linked to childhood or adolescent depression, something along the lines of "depressed adults feel sad, while depressed children feel angry." However, the more I have experienced depression in my own life and in my work as a clinician, the more I have seen the symptoms of irritability and anger as predominant features of depression.

Research published in the *Asian Journal of Psychiatry* shows that anger and depression are linked by how we handle our emotions. "People are more likely to express the angry or irritable signs in depression if they are individuals who tend to ruminate on past angry situations, or if they have difficulty in tempering their emotions," the researchers reported. "Those who are already quick to anger due to their temperament, culture, or upbringing, for instance, would also be more predisposed to express their depression through anger."[1]

Irritability creeps into our mind in a similar way that depression leads to difficulty concentrating and focusing. For example, consider all of the various functions your brain is engaged in at any given moment. Now think of depression coming in and reducing your brain's functioning capacity—your brain's capacity, which may typically be 95 percent when things are going well, is reduced to 60 percent.

So you're left with a brain that still has *a lot* of work to do but not as much capacity to do those things well. Now, say, your kid spills a cup of water. On a good day, when your brain is functioning at 95 percent, you're able to regulate your reaction to the situation. You take the spill in stride and say, "No big deal, here's a towel, let me fill that cup back up for you."

When you're depressed, however, your brain doesn't have the resources to regulate your reaction, and that same spilled glass of water can lead to a negative remark to your child and disregard of their reaction to your irritability. The next thing you know, your kid has run off to their room in tears, and you're left feeling guilty about the way you reacted.

It's a tough place to find ourselves. But we can learn to stop and take an inventory of our mood. Perhaps we find that we're depressed and haven't addressed that depression. And we might be able to use coping skills to address the depression that allows us to recover our focus, work through the irritability, and move forward in a healthy way.

So What Do We Do?

We have to be willing to put in a little work to move ourselves in the right direction, and that can be *really* hard when we're feeling depressed. A good first step is to make up our mind that we're done with our irritability causing problems for ourselves, our relationships, our family, and our life. Next, we begin the important work of exploring and restructuring our thought patterns to move us in a better direction.

Keeping a diary of our emotions and our reactions to those emotions is a great place to start. But if that seems like a high bar, consider pulling out one sheet of paper just to get things going. Look back on a situation, slow it down, and examine what exactly happened: I walked in the door, my kid spilled the spaghetti sauce, and I got frustrated. How can we possibly break that down any further?

While it all happened very fast, there is always an opportunity for deeper reflection and examination into the details. We might ask ourselves: *What is it that has led to my irritability? Is this because I'm depressed and trying to stuff that feeling down rather than address it? What am I thinking in that situation? Does my child spilling spaghetti sauce make me irritated because I have to clean it up? Does it make me think I'm not a good enough parent because I should have taught him how to slowly stir? What was my reaction to those thoughts, and was it warranted by the situation? What were the consequences of this situation? How did my child react, and what emotions did that reaction bring up inside of me?*

We draw this all out on paper, examine what was *really* behind our emotional response, and then explore different ways of thinking that will restructure our reactions and response. *And we write these down!* Simply thinking about these things isn't going to help. The whole point is to get them out of our head and onto paper so we can work them out. Consider it an emotional "show your work" kind of exercise.

We should work on this skill repeatedly until we're able to do this automatically. We want to move from reflecting back after an event and realizing our depression was triggering our irritable reaction and how we could have handled this better, to being able to pick up our depression's reaction to a situation on the fly and modify our thoughts and approach as we move through it. We want to build our strength in this approach to the point of being able to stop ourselves in the moment and think, *Wait, why am I irritable? Why do I have a decreased frustration tolerance right now?* Then, after a really brief introspective process, we can catch that the *real* reason for our irritability is our depressed mood, and we can interject coping skills for our depression to stave off our irritability.

Is There Healing and Relief Out There?

We are never locked into our irritable responses or our depressed mood forever, even though it often feels like that. Ultimately, we have control over our response and behaviors, even when depression and irritability take hold of us. It takes work, effort, *and* self-compassion. A big step toward finding healing and relief is to have a compassionate response to our own suffering.

When we're experiencing depression and the decreased ability to tolerate frustration that comes with it, *we are suffering*. And since we would most definitely be compassionate toward a friend, coworker, or loved one who was suffering, why shouldn't we be compassionate toward ourselves and our own suffering?

Researchers studying self-compassion as a coping tool for depression described self-compassion as a multistep process:

- Visualize yourself from the perspective of a compassionate observer.
- Notice from the outside how feelings are upsetting you and how they are reflected in your appearance.
- Try to let the warm feeling of compassion and desire to help arise within you.
- Say to yourself: "It is understandable that you feel that way. You are experiencing a natural response to depressing thoughts. But I am going to help you."
- Encourage yourself by saying: "You can pull yourself out of this mood again. You have already accomplished so much; you will be able to deal with this."
- Visualize putting your hand on your shoulder or hugging yourself to soothe and comfort yourself. Give yourself a friendly smile.
- Think about if there are other things you want to tell yourself that would energize and encourage you to cheer up.

- Take your time to say those things. When you feel it is appropriate, begin saying goodbye to yourself and remind yourself that you can come back every time you want.[2]

Some of this might sound a bit corny, but we *can* take steps toward healing, thinking better, remaining calm, increasing our frustration tolerance, and improving our mood by openly exploring and restructuring our thoughts. And similar to the aforementioned writing exercise, we should do these practices *out loud*. When we say things out loud or write them down on paper or in our phones, we can hear and see the results, and it goes a long way to reinforcing the work.

There will be times where these coping skills, self-compassion techniques, and cognitive restructuring won't be enough, and we should feel open to exploring the possibility of using medication, thoughtfully guided by a medical professional, to help us. If you're finding yourself overcome with irritability and a decreased ability to tolerate frustration because of depression, and you've tried various coping skills but find they haven't helped you move toward health and wellness, talk to your doctor about the potential need for medication. Even temporarily, medication can help us get over the hump at times. Realizing that we need that help is a sign of great strength, not weakness, as our stigmatizing society may make it seem.

What the Bible Says about Irritability

> Better is the end of a thing than its beginning;
> better is a patient spirit than a lofty one.
> Do not let anger upset your spirit,
> for anger lodges in the bosom of a fool.
> Do not say: How is it that former times were better than these? For it is not out of wisdom that you ask about this.
>
> —Ecclesiastes 7:8–10

One misconception in our secular culture is that the Christian faith pretends that everything will work out fine if we just pray and believe enough. When we look closely at the way the Bible addresses difficulties in our spiritual and emotional life, though, we find quite the opposite. In reality, scripture almost always states that these difficulties and struggles are going to come up in our lives no matter how much we believe and pray, and then it reminds us to take it seriously and figure out a course of action to cope with these experiences.

When it comes to irritability, scripture guides us to take stock of where we're at and then plan for healthy ways to move forward with positive coping. Proverbs 15:1 points to the power of the words we choose and how they can drive our emotions and behavior: "A harsh word stirs up anger." Most of us know from experience that the harsh thoughts and words we use about ourselves lead to deeper and darker depression. Instead, we should work to keep our thoughts and self-talk mild and reasonable.

We can't always trust our conclusions about how things are going. We always tend to think things were better in the past: *How did I end up like this? What did I do to deserve being in this situation?* But does pining for the past, which obviously looks better when we're mired in a depressing and difficult time, do anything for us? Was it actually as good as it looks from this point in our lives? Probably not. Instead of focusing on what we had, how life was better before X happened, it's far better for our emotional and spiritual health to reflect on the words of St. Paul: "Whatever is true, whatever is honorable, whatever is just, whatever is pure, whatever is lovely, whatever is gracious, if there is any excellence and if there is anything worthy of praise, think about these things" (Phil 4:8).

Changing the focus of our thinking is key when trying to battle against depression and the irritability that inevitably rears its ugly head. You've probably heard people suggest keeping a gratitude list to help you feel more positive, much along the same lines as St. Paul's advice. It works.

And as St. Paul writes in 1 Corinthians 10:13, God always provides a way out, a path toward healing and peace in our minds and hearts. It may not be the way out we've been hoping and praying for—for me, it's typically something like, "Just fix this for me, God" or "Please just cure me from this affliction *now*, thanks"—but it's always there. Sometimes that way out might be a compassionate friend, an opportunity to teach yourself some self-compassion, or slowing things down in order to respond in a manner that is more in line with the person you are.

What the Saints Say about Irritability

> The kingdom of God is peace in the Holy Spirit; He will reign in you if your heart is at peace. So, be at peace, Mademoiselle, and you will honor in a sovereign way the God of peace and love.
>
> —St. Vincent de Paul

There have been some irritable saints who have struggled in ways I can relate to. St. Jerome was known to carry around a stone that he would hit himself with every time he lost his temper.[3] St. James, the son of Zebedee, had "a reputation for temper, wanting to call down fire and brimstone on a Samaritan town which would not accept them."[4] And let's not forget Dorothy Day. James Forest, a Catholic Worker editor, once remarked, "She's not all sugar. See, she's tough, she's stubborn, she doesn't listen well all the time, she holds grudges, and like the other Catholic radicals, she has a problem about sometimes being too judgmental." Despite that critique, he considered her "a genius and a saint."[5]

I feel better just reading about them!

One of those saints I find consolation for in my irritability is St. Vincent de Paul. Born to peasant farmers in 1581 in France, he had a rocky life that included attending a university that was embroiled in literal armed battles and murder, being kidnapped by Barbary pirates, getting sold off as a slave, and experiencing two years in captivity.[6]

Despite all of that, Vincent connected with the Daughters of Charity about ten years after his slavery ordeal and began working with poor families. Thus began his long history of charity and love of the poor, which continues to this day via the Society of St. Vincent de Paul and all the wonderful work they continue to do in his name.

And . . . he was irritable. Omar F. A. Gutiérrez wrote of St. Vincent de Paul: "What did they say about him? Well, they said that he was 'by nature of a bilious temperament and very subject to anger.' When someone throws out a word like 'bilious' to describe you, you've got issues."[7]

But there was a key to Vincent's success that all of us can consider and contemplate as we battle our own irritability amid depression: "[Vincent] said that except for the grace of God he would have been 'hard and repulsive, rough and cross.' But he became a tender and affectionate man, very sensitive to the needs of others."[8]

God will always provide a way out, St. Paul reminds us (1 Cor 10:13). The grace of God that pours into our hearts, even without us realizing it, pulls us toward working on our depression and irritability. When we feel a tug toward trying a new coping skill to help us through our trials and mental health experiences, that's God's love and mercy right there. He's always there, pushing us along in ways we fail to recognize, bringing people into our lives to walk alongside us at exactly the right moment, and all we have to do is grasp the opportunity as St. Vincent de Paul did.

IN BRIEF

- Persistent irritability is a common symptom of depression.
- When we're depressed, our brain doesn't have its usual capacity to regulate emotional reactions.
- Keeping a diary of our emotions and reactions to those emotions is an effective coping tool.
- It is helpful to write down what was *really* behind our emotional response to a situation and then explore different ways of thinking to restructure future reactions and responses.
- We are never locked into our irritable responses or our depressed mood forever, even though it often feels like that.

CLOSING PRAYER

Let nothing perturb you. . . . All things pass. God does not change. Patience achieves everything.

—St. Teresa of Avila

3. FATIGUE

LORD, THE ONE YOU LOVE IS TIRED

We tend to put our physical health and mental health in two separate boxes, and yet our physical health and mental health are intertwined. A brief and random heart palpitation can trigger a panic attack. A deficiency in vitamin D levels in our body can drastically lower our mood. Being in a constant state of anxiety can put stress on our heart and increase our blood pressure.

And being depressed can make us drop-dead tired.

While we might think feeling normal again is as simple as getting a good night's sleep, the impact depression has on our energy levels can be much more complex to unwind.

When Depression Leaves You with Nothing Left in the Tank

When we're depressed, we lack motivation and feelings of self-efficacy. Overall, we're just wiped out. How in the world are we supposed to work on developing coping skills if we don't even have the energy to get out of bed?

Research indicates that more than 90 percent of those diagnosed with major depression disorder report the symptom of fatigue.[1] And it's not something we can just suck up and get over, as our culture often advises. Depression leaves us feeling as if our tank is empty not because we're feeling bad about ourselves but rather because of what's happening chemically in our brain. As Paige Smith reports on *HuffPost*, because depression affects the chemicals in our brain related to alertness and reward, "that means the illness physiologically has an impact on your energy levels."[2]

Someone who is feeling fatigued because of depression just can't decide to stop being tired. Saying it isn't easy to overcome sluggish neurotransmitters is an understatement. If you're experiencing this kind of intense decrease in motivation and energy, therapy alone can even have a hard time making an impact, which is why medication is worth considering.

I tell people this directly when they come in for therapy. When we're so depressed that we're unable to get out of bed, so depressed that we can barely make it through our morning routine without wanting to collapse back into bed, so depressed that we don't even have the motivation to take care of ourselves, how in the world is therapy going to work? Therapy requires *some* motivation, some interest. If intense depression inhibits that drive, we should most definitely consider medication first.

Medication for depression, even short term, can often be a crucial first step to feeling better. It can help us sleep better, provide a small boost of energy, and return those feelings of motivation that we can't remember having in the past. That support can help us start the work in therapy and get our mood back on track.

So What Do We Do?

Talking to a medical professional about medication and other potential underlying causes of our mental health symptoms—for example, vitamin D deficiency or thyroid issues—is one step we can take toward jump-starting our brain to fight fatigue caused by depression. Once we have that little bit of energy and motivation, we can start tackling the coping skills provided through therapy.

Realistically, though, I know a lot of us aren't going to want to turn toward medication for this issue, and that's OK. Generations of stigma toward taking medications for mental health have colored our view of treatment. Add to that the basic fact that it can be hard to access mental health services in today's world and we're more likely to try some simple strategies at home first.

So, let's go through some basics, such as eating healthy food. I know, I know—I can't imagine wanting to eat healthy food when I'm depressed either. I just want to drown my sorrows in candy and junk food, or maybe I don't want to eat at all. Yet science has shown again and again how nutrient-dense food can contribute to an improvement in our mood and energy levels. As reported on the website Psych Central, to combat fatigue caused by depression and the related loss of appetite, the clinical psychologist Shoshana Bennett "suggested setting an alarm for every two to three hours. When it rings, eat protein and a complex carbohydrate and drink water to stabilize your mood."[3]

While we know that depression can make it difficult to get a good's night sleep, there is something to be said for having a routine. Going to bed and waking up at scheduled times, avoiding screen time an hour before we want to go to bed, and developing a bedtime ritual—taking a shower, saying a specific set of prayers, and the like—can help our mind slow down and prepare for getting to bed and getting rest.

In fact, fighting what our depressed and fatigued brain is telling us to do is the crux of pushing back on our decreasing mood. This is true with eating, sleeping, and pushing ourselves to socialize when we don't feel like it. Sometimes when we're depressed, socializing can seem like this insurmountable mountain, and we've got absolutely zero energy to try to get to the summit. But it doesn't have to be that way. Texting, phone calls, video chats, or sitting on a park bench and just being around people whom we don't even socialize with can help our brain start to climb out of the darkest of holes.

One final point I'd like to bring to you is about adjusting our expectations. As one writer put it, "I have to continually—like four times a day—readjust my expectations. . . . If I can bring my expectations down, then I feel OK about myself. However, once I start comparing [myself] with other writers and people I respect, I'm in trouble."[4] Imagine how much better our lives would be if we adjusted our expectations to be more realistic rather than setting ourselves up for failure because we expect everything to be perfect.

Is There Healing and Relief Out There?

When we're suffering through depression and in a place where we're so fatigued we can't even bring ourselves to complete our usual daily tasks, it can feel like there's no hope. If we go to therapy and the therapist gives us a bunch of homework to do to help rewire our thinking, but we take it home and find we don't have the motivation or energy to work on it, we can feel there's no point.

But *there is healing and relief out there!*

Setting a therapy appointment and doing the homework *are* important and worth the work it takes to make them happen. (When you're suffering, you can always ask someone else to research doctors and help you get an appointment.) But there's something else you can do right now from the comfort of your own home to help you cope with depression fatigue: you can speak to yourself with compassion.

> Beating yourself up about being tired or calling yourself lazy only exacerbates the fatigue. . . . Pay attention to your negative self-talk. When you're feeling bad about yourself, consider "What am I saying to myself right now?". . . Then apologize and counter critical statements with the truth. Be specific[:] "I'm sorry. I didn't deserve that. I'm doing the best I can. This isn't laziness. I have a real illness. I'm taking good steps to help myself, such as attending therapy, drinking water and moving my body. I look forward to getting myself back."[5]

We must be gentle with ourselves. When I was in graduate school to become a therapist, one of the requirements was to go to therapy myself so I could experience it from the perspective of one seeking help. The first therapist I met with was also an expert in linguistics, the origins of language and specifically the etymology of words. When I would explain what was going on in my life, she would interrupt to ask why I chose the specific word I used, and she would help me understand what that word actually meant and then work to choose a more precise word that more accurately described what I was trying to get at. This taught me that the way we talk about ourselves changes the way we feel. Persistent negative self-talk truly shapes the way we see ourselves. Trying to give ourselves the benefit of the doubt and assume good intentions in our self-talk can move us in a better direction.

Working through negative self-talk is more than a mental exercise. We *must* get these things out of our mind and on to paper (or our phone). The A-B-C practice from cognitive behavioral therapy is a great way to look at how events (A) can trigger faulty and unhealthy thoughts (B) and then see what those thoughts do to us (C). For example, let's say I burn dinner. The first thought (A) that comes into my mind is, "I'm no good at taking care of my family; I can't even make a simple meal!" Of course, things don't end there. I end up taking that thought and letting it drive my behavior (B) in the immediate future. Once I think that I'm no good at taking care of my family, I quickly become more likely to avoid other tasks I'm asked to take on to help support my family. Perhaps my son comes to me and asks for help with his homework, and because I've decided "I'm no good at taking care of my family," I feel I can't help him with his homework and I avoid it altogether (C).

It doesn't take much to see how this negative self-talk spirals into self-destructiveness in our lives. When we're feeling too fatigued to take care of our basic responsibilities, the negative self-talk kicks into high gear and the consequences of that self-talk continue to push us deeper and deeper into depression. However, once we identify negative self-talk and the behaviors that result with the A-B-C process, we can replace that irrational belief with a rational one. It's completely irrational to decide that I'm unable to care for my family just because I burned dinner. Burning dinner happens to the best of us, and the reasons dinner was ruined could be because I was distracted, the oven runs too hot, or the recipe I looked up online was incorrect. Whatever the reason, just because dinner is burned doesn't mean I can't pull out leftovers and adjust our plans for the night's meal. The burned dinner doesn't necessarily say anything bad about me. Once we learn to incorporate these more rational thoughts into our process, we can avoid the unhealthy consequences of the negative self-talk.

The more we practice this method on paper, the more rapid and automatic we can become at catching our irrational thoughts and coming up with more rational explanations on the fly. And over time, replacing negative self-talk with more reasonable and positive self-talk will start to push us in a more energizing direction.

What the Bible Says about Being Fatigued

> Be gracious to me, Lord, for I am in distress;
> affliction is wearing down my eyes,
> my throat and my insides.
> My life is worn out by sorrow,
> and my years by sighing.
> My strength fails in my affliction;
> my bones are wearing down.
>
> —Psalm 31:10–11

God doesn't hide from acknowledging the difficulties we will face in life. There is never a message of "Life is going to be great for those who love me." Instead, there's a steady recognition of the suffering we will all face and a hopeful plan for how to start taking steps in the right direction despite this suffering.

Unfortunately, one of the most common replies we'll get when we tell our Catholic friends that we're feeling depressed is that we should pray for healing. Of course, Christ hears our prayers, especially those when we're suffering, and of course he can give us healing from our suffering with just the request being sent his way. But depression hits us even in the depths of our souls—"My soul is depressed," says Psalm 119:28. The idea that we can just pick up and pray for peace and healing when our soul is depressed feels almost as ridiculous as being told to "suck it up and get through your sadness by pulling yourself up by the bootstraps!" Sometimes it just isn't happening.

Our Lord says, "Come to me, all you who labor and are burdened, and I will give you rest" (Mt 11:28). With Christ there is rest, comfort, and healing from all our suffering. All our depression and fatigue finds healing through Christ. But *how* do we come to him? Some take this passage to mean that all we have to do is pray and we will be healed, but that's definitely not how Christ meant it. We know this precisely because Christ himself prayed for suffering to pass over him and to be spared, and he wasn't (see Matthew 26:36–44). He opened himself up to the will of God, even though it went against his preferences, and it wasn't the will of God for him to be spared.

For those of us suffering from depression and fatigue, Christ asks us to come to him through the community of his Body—those loved ones, our friends and family, who can pray for us and help us connect to mental health services when we're unable to do so on our own; those healing professionals who can help us with medication if it's needed and teach us coping skills through therapy to fight back against depression. And Christ continues to come to us through his Church, his sacraments, and the holy men and women who have answered his call to vocations to the priesthood and religious life. Remember, our faith is one of incarnation—Christ will give us rest if we come to him; he just might not be trying to come to us in the way we might think.

What the Saints Say about Being Fatigued

> You will be consoled according to the greatness of your sorrow and affliction; the greater the suffering, the greater will be the reward.
>
> —St. Mary Magdalene de' Pazzi

Believe it or not, the saints got tired! I'm not just saying the saints got tired and needed to get a good night's sleep every now and then. Many saints got tired from depression and responsibilities, and sometimes they wanted to pull the covers over the heads and not come out, just like us.

One of those saints was Mary Magdalene de' Pazzi. Mary was born into one of the wealthiest families in Florence, Italy, in 1566, but she quickly focused her sights on other things, learning to meditate on the Passion of Christ, practicing mortification of the flesh, receiving First Communion, making a vow of virginity, and experiencing her first spiritual ecstasy between the ages of nine and twelve.[6]

She once said, "Those who call to mind the sufferings of Christ, and who offer up their own to God through his passion, find their pains sweet and pleasant."[7] However, her strong devotion to the suffering of Christ opened her up to receive suffering from him, meant to be offered up for the sins of the world. She felt that suffering when she was nineteen when "she started five years of dryness and desolation in which she was tempted to sin, and she didn't even want to pray. In her darkness everything in life seemed horrible and gloomy. She was so depressed that twice she came close to suicide. All she could do to fight this darkness was to serve others, help others, hold on to prayer, and trust God."[8]

Just like that, Mary Magdalene de' Pazzi becomes someone we can reach, someone we can feel connected to, even though her holiness seems to put her out of our orbit. She becomes for all of us a saint we can ask to intercede for us because she knows what it is to feel depressed, fatigued, and hopeless. She reminds us that we "will be consoled according to the greatness of your sorrow and affliction." No matter how dark our lives get, we can look to the crucifix as Mary Magdalene de' Pazzi did and find hope.

IN BRIEF

- Fatigue can sneak up on us as a symptom of depression we don't often recognize.
- Depression doesn't leave us feeling like our tank is empty just because we're feeling bad about ourselves; it's because of what's happening chemically in our brains.
- Therapy requires *some* motivation, some interest. If we don't have it in the moment because of intense depression, we should consider medication as a first step.
- Persistent negative self-talk shapes the way we see ourselves. Giving ourselves the benefit of the doubt and assuming good intentions in our self-talk can move things in a better direction.
- For those of us suffering from depression and fatigue, Christ asks us to come to him through the community of his Body: in loved ones, in healing professionals, and in the Church and its sacraments and ministers.

CLOSING PRAYER

We must pray without tiring, for the salvation of mankind does not depend on material success; nor on sciences that cloud the intellect. Neither does it depend on arms and human industries, but on Jesus alone.

—St. Frances Xavier Cabrini

4. HOPELESSNESS

LORD, THE ONE YOU LOVE DOESN'T WANT TO GO ON

There was nothing left for me. No reason to keep putting one foot in front of the other. No reason to get out of bed. No reason to pray, to eat, to live. This was the tape playing repeatedly in my mind after receiving a prenatal diagnosis that was incompatible with life for our son.

I wanted to die.

I prayed for death.

In God's infinite mercy, he didn't answer that prayer. But I was left heartbroken, soul shattered, and hopeless.

Unless you've experienced that kind of hopelessness, it's hard to imagine it. In my situation, it wouldn't be unfair to wonder how I could feel so completely hopeless. I had a home, a job, three healthy and happy children, a wonderful wife, and a community that was supportive in the face of our suffering.

But my mind and my hopelessness didn't care about my blessings.

When you're on the other side of an experience like that, it's tempting to look back and think about what kept you from ending it all—if I wanted to die, what was the reason I didn't become overwhelmed by that feeling and take those steps? It's easy to consider all the aforementioned blessings as protective factors that kept me alive long enough to write this book. However, when you consider the intense out-of-this-world pain that hopelessness brings, I think it's perhaps more reasonable to see the protective factor as something equally out of this world.

As we sat in the first row of our son's funeral, about four months after receiving his diagnosis, the priest shared something I will never forget: "It's easy to look at this situation and conclude that all of our prayers did nothing. But I see that all our prayers were used by God to keep this family going, to keep them alive." He went on to point out that this experience should have destroyed us, leaving us completely unable to continue on with our lives. And yet here we were, broken but not defeated, hopeless but not dead. The priest offered that God took the prayers of everyone we knew, everyone praying for a miracle, and perhaps performed a miracle that we weren't recognizing: we were still alive, still walking forward through our dark valley. We were still here.

"My Only Friend Is Darkness"

When we're feeling depressed, we're sure to hear, "Everything is going to be OK," or "We know that all things work for good for those who love God." Is everything going to be OK, though? Is this helpful to say to someone who's experiencing depression? Hearing that God would somehow bring good out of my son's death certainly didn't help me. I mean, I know that it's true, but it sure didn't feel like it in the moment, and hearing it again and again from Catholic friends actually made me angry because it never felt like the promised good would ever outweigh the bad.

Our faith communities tend to focus on the hope we can find in Christ no matter how dark our lives may appear at any moment. After all, in Hebrews 11:1 we read, "Faith is the realization of what is hoped for and evidence of things not seen." In Romans 5:1–2, St. Paul writes, "Therefore, since we have been justified by faith, we have peace with God through our Lord Jesus Christ, through whom we have gained access [by faith] to this grace in which we stand, and we boast in hope of the glory of God." We also have the very fact of the Resurrection after the suffering and death of Christ on the Cross. In fact, the entire Christian faith is founded on hope in times of darkness, and Christ himself is proof of the truth of that hope.

However, despite the hope offered by our faith, it's hard to describe exactly how it feels to be so depressed that we're completely hopeless.

Psalm 88:19 seems to do about as good a job as I've ever found: "My only friend is darkness." And when I have found myself feeling this way, I don't usually respond well to hopeful platitudes. It's hard to pinpoint why that is exactly, but I think there's a connection to something I've learned as a husband. Early in my marriage, if my wife told me something wasn't going right—difficulties at her work, problems around the house, even emotional experiences that were hard to get through—I would instantly want to figure out how to fix it. But that wasn't what she wanted. She wanted someone to listen, to understand her experience, and to be there for her. That's it. Once I accepted the role she needed me to play, I found it quite liberating, and she felt more supported.

When I think about how I feel when I'm hopeless and what kind of support I'm looking for, I feel this exact same way. I don't want someone to fix my hopelessness—to recount all the ways that things are going to work out, that God loves me, or that hope is there even though I don't see it. I just want someone to hear what I'm going through, acknowledge it, try to understand it with empathy, and walk with me through the journey.

So What Do We Do?

When we feel hopeless, the first step is to cut ourselves some slack. The crippling feelings of hopelessness are a symptom of depression; they are something that happens to our brain without our consent. We must free ourselves of the guilt that we may experience because of our hopelessness. Thoughts like *I should know better* or *Christ gives me hope, so how can I possibly feel like this?* feed our negative perception of ourselves and make us believe our depression is our fault. And that's not true.

However, just because something is a symptom that came upon us without our consent *does not mean* we're helpless to fight against it. In fact, we can control our thinking, which leads us to strengthen our resolve over moods and emotional states in general. It just takes practice and realistic small-goal setting.

One way to practice controlling our thinking is to imagine a bridge, with depression on one side and relief on the other. Right now, we're on the depression side, and it can feel impossible to get to the other side. However, the first step is not to get on the other side of the bridge but rather to step onto the bridge. We do that by recognizing how our thoughts of hopelessness worsen how we already feel. Once we acknowledge how these thoughts are harming us, we can work to correct them by questioning them—for example, asking if it's *really true* that nothing could ever improve our situation—and by seeing if we are making predictions about the future that might be incorrect.[1]

This process of questioning our thoughts and predictions is crucial to fighting back against our depression and battling our hopelessness. It is precisely by taking our hopeless thoughts and playing them out that we can start to see they are lies. Once we recognize that our hopelessness is a lie, or at the very least it's not the complete truth, hopelessness loses its power over us. Just by asking "Is it true that nothing in the next three years could possibly happen that would change this situation?" and arriving at even a weak answer such as "OK, well, *maybe* something could happen to change my thoughts on my life," we have knocked back the power of hopelessness and started to move in a healthier direction.

Is There Healing and Relief Out There?

While I'm the first to recommend suffering alongside people and walking with them through their darkness as the best way to help them, I want to remind those suffering from depression and hopelessness that there are steps we can take to start fighting back.

The mental battle against hopelessness comes down to what psychologists call cognitive distortions, which are the ways that our mind tries to make us believe things that aren't accurate.[2] Many times our thoughts get stuck in certain cognitive distortions, and certain kinds of therapy—specifically cognitive behavioral therapy—focus on helping us realize these thoughts as being irrational and unhealthy. We must learn what distortions are impacting us and then use different skills to help us develop healthier ways of looking at the world.

There are many cognitive distortions, but in terms of battling against hopelessness, we'll focus on personalization and polarized thinking. Personalization is a cognitive distortion where we start to believe that everything that happens is somehow related to us. Whatever people do, whatever they say, and whatever happens in our lives and the lives of those around us—everything is somehow connected and directly related to us. We think we are personally responsible for everything happening when in reality it's outside of our control. An example could be getting a flat tire and immediately thinking, *This is my fault for not paying more attention to my car.* Another example: our child gets sick and we think, *This is my fault for not being a good parent.*

When combating personalization, we work on what is known as reattribution, which involves exploring what has happened and working to find other reasons outside of ourselves for the event.[3] Our car got a flat tire because there was a nail in the road that we randomly happened to run over. Our child got sick because kids get sick all the time and school is basically a living germ factory. Once we start to see that not everything is because of something we've done or not done, we can start to see the world more realistically and rationally and free ourselves from feeling responsible and hopeless.

Polarized thinking, also known as all-or-nothing thinking or black-and-white thinking, is one of the most common cognitive distortions we all tend to struggle with. This cognitive distortion leads us to see everything as either/or. We're either healthy or a disgusting wreck. We're either joyful and happy or depressed and hopeless. We're either holy and headed to heaven or a sinner unworthy of God's mercy.

When our thinking is polarized, it's easy for us to fall into feelings of hopelessness precisely because we conclude that we're going to either be depressed forever or feel happy and hopeful. It's that inability to live in the middle—sometimes we're going to feel good and sometimes we're going to feel bad, and that's okay—where hopelessness can be found.

When we feel depressed or hopeless, we may also feel all alone, as though no one can understand what we're going through. A good way to battle this feeling of alienation comes from Therese J. Borchard, a well-known advocate for mental health awareness:

> Many who feel alienated assume (wrongly) that absolutely no one is, or ever will be, in their corner. The antidote for mind reading is to examine the emotional evidence. This requires courage in the form of trust and openness to survey how others actually experience you.
>
> If you feel forsaken, it is important to get outside of your head to see if your inner reality is an accurate reflection of the outside world. Most people who feel forsaken are overgeneralizing from a relatively small sample of experiences. With more extensive sampling, it is highly likely that they will encounter more hope-promoting responses from others. The antidote to all-or-nothing thinking is thinking in shades of gray—opening oneself up to the continuum of possibilities for one's life.[4]

The fight against polarized thinking lies in actively thinking in terms of both/and instead of either/or, which thankfully is something that comes naturally to Catholics. We often experience and live out our faith in that world of both/and, and that helps us transition that same idea to our emotional health.

Life is rarely all or nothing, black or white; it's almost always gray. Good things can still happen to us when we're depressed; bad things can still happen to us when we're feeling well.

In the months after the death of our son, I was firmly planted in my belief that *all* aspects of my life were awful and *nothing* would ever get better again. That trap, that cognitive distortion, held me firmly in hopelessness and depression. However, we were living through this experience with three young children running around the house. While they all certainly experienced the loss of their brother and felt sad or angry at different times, they also felt joyful, silly, and loving at other times.

Our children embodied the healthier thought process that dragged me away from my cognitive distortion. I could experience heartbreak and hopelessness while experiencing joy and happiness. It didn't come easy. It often felt like a betrayal of our son's memory to laugh and have fun, but looking back I see that's the cognitive distortion desperately hanging on to me and my emotions. As the kids continued to bring that light into my darkness, the cognitive distortion lost its grip. I was able to see that things were grayer than I realized, and that helped me heal and take some steps forward in the grieving process.

What the Bible Says about Hopelessness

> For in hope we were saved. Now hope that sees for itself is not hope. For who hopes for what one sees? But if we hope for what we do not see, we wait with endurance.
>
> In the same way, the Spirit too comes to the aid of our weakness; for we do not know how to pray as we ought, but the Spirit itself intercedes with inexpressible groanings.
>
> —Romans 8:24–26

Have you ever taken the time to sit down and read the book of Job? The insights in the book of Job are profound, and even just the experience of reading along as someone struggles with hope and the trials of his life can be healing.

"Where then is my hope, my happiness, who can see it?" (Jb 17:15). I've thought this exact same thing during my dark valleys, and to see it in the Bible gives me a grain of hope in my hopelessness. The Bible continually shows us examples of people just like us who are suffering, questioning, and wondering where we're supposed to find hope in a hopeless situation. God doesn't expect us to feel hopeful all the time; he knows we can't. Instead, he helps us to know that he understands why we wouldn't feel hopeful in every situation, and that brings me peace.

Probably the most important thing we can read about hopelessness in the Bible, though, comes from the scene of Jesus in the Garden, when our Lord and Savior says, "My soul is sorrowful even to death" (Mt 26:38). It's clear that Jesus was filled with sorrow, an intense sorrow that we can clearly relate to in our times of depression and hopelessness. The Son of God reached up to God the Father in prayer for relief and peace amid heartache and distress, just like you and me.

It's painful. It's beautiful. It's exactly the connection to our God that we all need in our own moments of suffering.

What the Saints Say about Hopelessness

> The saints did not all begin well, but they ended well.
> —St. John Vianney

When I'm not feeling well, my mind quickly races to the point where I feel I'll never end up well. It seems like I'm on a road destined for failure. But picturing the words of St. John Vianney and applying them to my own depression and hopelessness reminds me of the need to fight such polarized thinking.

Another incredible example of fighting polarized thinking comes to us from holy hero Bl. Clara Isabella Fornari. Born in 1697 in Rome, Clara was close to God from the very beginning of her life and entered the Poor Clares at the young age of fifteen. After making her vows with the order, Clara began to have mystical experiences, including visions of Jesus, Mary, St. Clare of Assisi (who started the order she had joined), and St. Catherine of Siena.

During one of her encounters with Christ, Clara shared that our Lord placed a ring on her finger and referred to her as his "spouse of sorrow."[5] From that point, Clara's life was anything but easy. She experienced the stigmata, was thrown down the stairs by the devil, and had to fight against evil forces that were intent on destroying her faith:[6] "Despite her nearness to God, Clara Isabella was tormented by despair and her physical pain. The devil taunted her relentlessly, making her wish to commit suicide and abandon her faith. This deep depression overwhelmed her completely. At times, she could not remember the beauty of her visions. Her joy returned right before her death."[7]

Bl. Clara Isabella Fornari suffered from depression, despair, and hopelessness yet found herself deeply and mystically connected to Christ through that suffering. She is a wonderful intercessor, ready and waiting to help all of us who need relief and peace from our sorrow. May her example help us to always remember that we can hope in Jesus Christ even in our darkest moments.

IN BRIEF

- Unless we've experienced hopelessness, it's hard to imagine it.
- When we're hopeless, our typical first attempt at coping is to give up. Spoiler: it doesn't work.
- Thoughts such as *I should know better* or *If Christ gives me hope, how can I possibly feel like this?* feed our negative perception of ourselves and make our depression seem like our fault, which is not true.
- Ask yourself, "Is it true that nothing in the next three years could possibly happen that would change this situation?" It is precisely by taking our hopeless thoughts and playing them out that we can start to see they are lies.
- Our mind uses cognitive distortion to make us believe things that aren't accurate. Certain kinds of therapy, specifically cognitive behavioral therapy, focus on helping us realize these thoughts are irrational and unhealthy.
- The Son of God felt sorrowful, just like you and me. The Son of God reached up to God the Father in prayer for relief and peace amid heartache and distress, just like you and me.

CLOSING PRAYER

> No one, however weak, is denied a share in the victory of the Cross. No one is beyond the help of the prayer of Christ.
>
> —St. Leo the Great

ANXIETY

5. ANXIETY

LORD, THE ONE YOU LOVE IS WORRYING

As I climbed back in bed after putting our newborn son down in his crib for the eighth time that night, I began to feel a wave of panic start in my head and pour throughout my body. I didn't understand what was happening. It was a feeling I had never experienced before. My heart began to race, my breathing rapidly shifted into what I would almost call hyperventilating, and my body began involuntarily shaking. My wife sat up and asked what was happening, and I couldn't explain it. I just lay in bed, shaking, panicking, and feeling as if my body was about to explode.

And then almost as quickly as it came and equally without an explanation or reason, it passed.

Ten years later, this event that lasted less than three minutes and was the only panic attack I've ever experienced is still burned into my mind. I remember that moment whenever I speak with someone who shares their experience of panic attacks, and I wish I could do something to help give them relief.

Over the years, the experience of anxiety has slowly morphed from a cluster of mental health symptoms into almost a part of my personality. I feel anxious so much of the time that I've pretty much conceded defeat; I no longer even think about trying to fight the symptoms. I just consider myself to be an "anxious person."

Am I Anxious or Just Worried?

Anxiety and generalized anxiety disorder can be tricky conditions to recognize we need help for. Most of us experience anxiety, and most of us decide to simply stop worrying so much. If only it were that easy.

If you've experienced anxiety in the past, you understand how its symptoms can be difficult to track. They come and go, we question if they were actually present, and we don't really tell anyone about them, so it's hard to reach out for help in gathering data. But similar to every other mental health condition, we need to seek help if the symptoms we are experiencing make it hard for us to carry out our day-to-day activities or responsibilities, cause problems in our relationships or at work, or make other areas of our life more difficult to engage in.

Another specific marker in deciding if your anxiety is cause for worry is to notice if you experience anxiety even when there's no specific threat or if your anxiety is out of proportion to the threat taking place. As an example, imagine your boss told you that your typical weekly meeting with them was canceled. This could cause *some* anxiety for any of us. We can imagine feeling worried because there was an issue we needed to bring up to them and we're concerned that we might forget before the rescheduled meeting takes place. However, if we start to spiral down into our anxiety—worrying that our job may be at risk because of this canceled meeting, that there's surely some reason unknown to us that the meeting was canceled but *we definitely know* the reason will have some catastrophic results on us and our employment—it's a safe bet that we're being excessive.

I often ask people who suffer from anxiety, "How do you know you're anxious? If you could look at yourself from the outside, what would you see that indicates that you're experiencing excessive anxiety?" Their responses help me as a therapist better understand the specific symptoms that need to be targeted. For an individual coming in for help, however, such questions can be baffling. Typically when we get asked something like this, our first response is, "I don't know, I'm just *really* anxious!"

Anxiety comes into our mind and body quickly, and it can be difficult to slow down and figure out what triggered it and how it will play out. But this can be crucial information in trying to work on coping skills and knowing when and how to employ them. So, if you've had a difficult time explaining what anxiety is like for you, consider some of the following common symptoms: worry that is challenging to control, edginess, restlessness, fatigue, difficulty concentrating or thinking clearly, irritability or decreased frustration tolerance, muscle aches, sleep disturbances, racing heart, headache, rapid breathing, hypervigilance, sweating, nausea, and even diarrhea.

It's important to get these symptoms out into the open, because all too often our friends and family members who have never experienced excessive, uncontrolled anxiety have no idea how intense it can be. It takes over your mind and body, and if it escalates into a panic attack, it can literally feel like you are about to die. Our loved ones want to be helpful but often believe it's a relatively minor intensity of distress and that we just need encouragement to get over it. Letting people know exactly how intense excessive anxiety can be will lead to reducing stigma and increasing compassion and caring.

So What Do We Do?

To cope with anxiety, we start with being willing to be vulnerable. Have you ever felt so alone in your symptoms, in your experience, that you flat-out decide there is absolutely no one on earth who knows what you're going through? All of us have. But have you ever shared your experience, even minimally, and come to find there's an entire community of people exactly like you, including people you never would have guessed would have that experience, and you end up finding a big support group out there that *gets you*?

People in the pews next to you at Mass experience anxiety and worry, *just like you*. The coworker you sit next to day in and day out experiences anxiety, *just like you*. The priest who leads your parish and looks as if he's got absolutely everything together experiences panic attacks from time to time, *just like you*. We're all out there, but because of the stigma associated with mental health symptoms and the intense desire to keep our true selves completely hidden, we're prevented from seeing one another, meeting one another, and ever knowing the power of walking alongside others in terms of their mental healing *and* ours.

I'm not suggesting that you should take it upon yourself to share your feelings with every person in the world. I'm not going to neighborhood parties and walking up to people saying, "Hi, I'm Tommy, and I suffer from crippling anxiety!" We have absolutely no obligation to share our mental health struggles with anyone at all. However, if we trust our instincts, we will find that we come across certain people we can trust, certain people who we know will accept us when we share our struggles, and that's where the benefit is. And in being open with our experiences, we also may help someone else.

Is There Healing and Relief Out There?

Support from others is helpful, but it can only go so far. Sometimes our anxiety can leave us needing to work on things all by ourselves. While medication for anxiety can be effective as a temporary help, it's the hard work of developing and practicing coping skills in therapy and on our own that leads us to peace amid the pain of anxiety.

Coping skills related to anxiety are most effective *before* our anxiety rises to the level of a panic attack. So it's important to learn how to recognize anxiety as it begins to form, understanding the patterns in our thinking or our daily life that jump-start anxiety, and then acting prior to the anxiety growing beyond that point of no return. Once we've shifted into a panic attack, we find that sometimes the only thing we can do is ride it out, which is terrifying and underscores all the more how important it is to develop a plan for prior to that point.

Breathing is the most well-known coping strategy for dealing with anxiety. Slowing down our breathing can help to slow down our mind, and it's a great place to begin. However, one of the main issues with anxiety is that we get stuck in our head, our mind begins to race, we start to think of all the worst possible outcomes, and before we know it—*boom!*—we're panicked. To calm our anxious mind, it's helpful to get out of our head and focus on the present moment. Take a walk and focus on the things you are experiencing with your senses. For example, on a "color walk," you try to find the colors of the rainbow in the order they appear in nature. Start by trying to find something natural that is red, then something orange, something yellow, and on through the end of the rainbow. A "five senses walk" is similar: go for a walk and focus on what you can hear, see, smell, feel, and taste (although that last one may be a little weird, depending on where you're taking your walk and whether you've brought snacks). Putting ourselves into the present, engaging our senses, and experiencing what is going on around us will help us escape the anxiety spiral that our negative thinking sends us into.

Therapy is also available to help us prepare for and get through our bouts with anxiety. It can be challenging to develop coping skills when we're in the midst of suffering. Therapy can help us pull together a wellness plan *when we're feeling healthy*, and then we can use those coping strategies when anxiety strikes. Therapy can also help us during those times when we can't figure out how to help ourselves. Even a brief course of treatment with a therapist can help us learn coping skills that we can use for the rest of our lives when faced with anxiety.

What the Bible Says about Anxiety

> Therefore I tell you, do not worry about your life, what you will eat [or drink], or about your body, what you will wear. Is not life more than food and the body more than clothing? Look at the birds in the sky; they do not sow or reap, they gather nothing into barns, yet your heavenly Father feeds them. Are not you more important than they? Can any of you by worrying add a single moment to your life-span?
>
> —Matthew 6:25–27

Our Lord and the Early Church recognized how big a struggle anxiety is for the human person. For Christ himself to repeatedly bring up the issue shows just how much he understood the complexities of our mental health and how deeply he wants to give us peace amid our struggles.

Taken out of context, many of the passages from scripture that refer to anxiety might be seen as thinking freedom from anxiety is easy to achieve. *You mean all I have to do is stop worrying, cast my worries on him, and just have no anxiety at all?!* Obviously it isn't that easy.

A better understanding would be that scripture is imploring us to take our anxiety seriously, to realize that it can be a stumbling block to our peace and tranquility, and to pray *and* act to challenge it, work through it, and find wellness.

As with everything else we read in scripture, the message must be framed within the context of the Cross, the Passion, and the Resurrection. Jesus could have chosen a painless and easy way to bring salvation to his people, but he didn't. Precisely because we needed to see it, God became man and lived a life filled with pain and sorrow to give us hope in our own lives, no matter how dark they become.

When we consider the Incarnation, the very fact that God became human to save us, we see that God works on us *through* others. Christianity is a community-based faith; it isn't simply about "me and Jesus." Instead, Christ comes to us and is truly present in the people around us. He comes in the guise of a loved one, a caring friend, a helping professional. And if we can find the strength to cast all our worries on him and on the various members who make up his Body here on earth, maybe we will be closer to feeling how much he cares for us and finding that peace we desperately desire.

What the Saints Say about Anxiety

> Pray, hope, and don't worry.
>
> —St. Padre Pio

The saints can so often feel beyond our reach. Their trust in God seems to hover at a level we will never attain, and they make everything seem so simple. That seems especially true with St. Padre Pio's mantra: "Pray, hope, and don't worry." It seems so easy, so simple, and yet when I pray and hope for an end to anxiety and worry, nothing happens.

Born in 1887 in Italy, Francesco Forgione was raised in a deeply religious family. As a child, he reported having visions and ecstasies, and at the young age of fifteen he donned the Franciscan habit and joined the Capuchins, taking the name Friar Pio in honor of Pope Pius I. Within two years, Pio began to get extremely ill, suffering from a loss of appetite, insomnia, exhaustion, fainting spells, migraines, and frequent vomiting.

Despite trying to live as a humble servant of the Lord, Pio become quite popular as it became clear he was a holy man close to the Lord. At one point, in an effort to slow down his increasing popularity, the Vatican imposed sanctions on him, including forbidding him from saying Mass, blessing people, answering letters, and communicating with his spiritual director.

While he was granted a great many spiritual experiences—the stigmata, bilocation, prophecy, healing, and apparitions—life was not easy for the Capuchin friar. And his now famous mantra of "Pray, hope, and don't worry," far from being a simplistic solution to our struggles with anxiety, was what he had to repeat to himself again and again to remind himself to stay focused on God's providence as a way of fighting against the anxiety he surely experienced.

Now, more than half a century after his death, St. Padre Pio stands as an advocate for all of us suffering from anxiety. He is a friend who understands and stands at the ready to intercede for us with Christ, begging him to pour his grace and peace into our hearts to give us that relief he so desperately wants us to experience.

So if you, like me, find yourself praying, hoping, and yet still experiencing worry and anxiety, reach out! Reach out to learn and develop coping skills to help you navigate the journey. Reach out to a helping professional who can guide you along the way to wellness. And reach out to Christ directly and through his saints!

IN BRIEF

- Worrying is excessive if the anxiety is present even when there's no specific threat or if it's out of proportion to the threat taking place.
- Common symptoms of anxiety include worry that is challenging to control, edginess, restlessness, fatigue, difficulty concentrating or thinking clearly, irritability or decreased frustration tolerance, muscle aches, sleep disturbances, racing heart, headache, rapid breathing, hypervigilance, sweating, nausea, and even diarrhea.
- Learning how to recognize anxiety as it begins to form, understanding the patterns in our thinking or our daily life that jump-start

anxiety, and then practicing coping tools prior to the anxiety going beyond that point of no return can help prevent anxiety from overwhelming us.

- Taking a walk and focusing on the things we are experiencing with our senses is an effective coping tool.
- Our Lord and the Early Church recognized how big a struggle anxiety is for us.

CLOSING PRAYER

Deliver us, Lord, we pray, from every evil, graciously grant peace in our days, that, by the help of your mercy, we may be always free from sin and safe from all distress, as we await the blessed hope and the coming of our Savior, Jesus Christ.

—The Embolism at Mass

6. SOCIAL ANXIETY

LORD, THE ONE YOU LOVE IS SELF-CONSCIOUS

All of us experience concerns and worry about what other people are thinking about us from time to time. We look to see if there's broccoli in our teeth after dinner, we check to make sure our zipper is firmly in place, and we ask our friend if our hair looks right, all because we want to put our best foot forward and not be seen as weird by others.

When one of those things happens to go wrong, we can find ourselves feeling anxious or embarrassed. But imagine feeling overwhelmed simply by the thought of having to interact with others, to feel certain that something was going to go wrong when you're around others, to the point of deciding it's better to just avoid everyone altogether. Imagine feeling anxiety and panic to the point of feeling like you might die of a heart attack when you're out and about in public. It's a totally different experience.

Social Anxiety Isn't Just Being Introverted

Many of us conceptualize our social unease and disinterest in socializing as a form of social anxiety. But true social anxiety is not the same as being introverted and shy around others.

The National Institute of Mental Health explains that social anxiety disorder is "an intense, persistent fear of being watched and judged by others."[1] It's a fear that has physical effects—nausea, rapid heart rate, and feeling our mind go blank—and can impact behavior, including keeping people from going places where there are other people.

Social anxiety is a serious mental health issue that requires intervention in order for people to live the life of peace they deserve. It's easy to understand how these symptoms perpetuate the anxiety into a spiral that seems to have no end. We start out anxious that we're going to be judged by others and then once we're around other people, we start to feel physically sick and our mind goes blank. We're asked a question and can't come up with an answer because of the symptoms we're feeling, and we immediately feel our fears about being judged by others are confirmed.

They're looking at me weird, they're thinking negative things about me, I'm in danger just by being around them: these are the common thoughts people with social anxiety might have that feed into behavior such as going to the grocery store at 2 a.m. because there will be fewer people there, staying home from family gatherings because we're less likely to feel embarrassed or awkward when we're alone, or even calling in sick to work or avoiding going to school because we're so panicked by the thought of someone asking us why we're blushing or sweating.

The problem here is that social support is exactly what we need.

So What Do We Do?

When it comes to social anxiety, worry, and persistent fears, the best way to work on them is not to avoid them but to confront them. I know what you're thinking: *Are you seriously suggesting that the ideal treatment for my fear and panic is to purposely put myself into the very situations that bring me that fear and panic?!*

"Some things are worth doing even if you're anxious," explains the psychologist Barbara Markway. "You will be amazed at what you can do while still feeling a lot of unpleasant sensations. Sometimes people will notice your anxiety; other times, they won't. Either way, you'll feel better about yourself if you go ahead and act—do what you value. As . . . psychologist Steven Hayes say[s], 'Be willing to stand in the hurricane and do what you think is important.'"[2]

"Be willing to stand in the hurricane"—that sounds terrifying, and it's not really the inspiring message I hope for when I'm riddled with anxiety. But it's the message we need to hear. When we find ourselves crippled by social anxiety to the point of no longer wanting to leave our home, we must act, and avoiding the anxiety-provoking situation by leaving home only at times that feel safe isn't going to cut it. Instead, we have to walk out into the hurricane: go grocery shopping at busier times, meet up with friends for coffee in public, and walk downtown where there are people all around.

In short, we must learn to tolerate uncertainty.

"This is a tough one," Markway explains. "Most people like things to be clear-cut—to know where things stand. Unfortunately, life doesn't always cooperate. You must eventually face the ugly truth that you can't control everything. Not everyone will like you. Not everyone will approve of your every action. Sometimes your best bet is to go with the flow and learn the gentle art of acceptance."[3]

We often try to control our social anxiety by not leaving our home, only being around people we feel we can trust, or any other means we can think of. But the anxiety continues and will continue until we realize that we simply cannot control everything. We can set things up as much as possible before engaging in an event that brings on anxiety and still things can happen that we didn't foresee.

When we walk into that hurricane, we must actively work to make it through the situation. Breathing to beat the anxiety, working on reframing our thinking and being more rational and realistic with our thoughts, and even closing our eyes and working to put ourselves in the present moment rather than allowing the spinning thoughts of anxiety to take over—these are tools to work through the situation. We can't expect that we'll just make it through an anxiety-provoking situation without actively fighting against it. We have to prepare, practicing these skills when we are in anxiety-provoking situations and when we're feeling okay.

It takes time and practice, but as we slowly make it through the social anxiety, our brain will begin to see that the worry and concern were ill placed, and we'll slowly move toward health and clearer thinking when it comes to these kinds of experiences.

Is There Healing and Relief Out There?

Social anxiety is overwhelming. A lot of times we can feel it's better to settle into our isolation rather than dealing with the seriously scary panic. After all, as I sit in my room and feel that fear as I consider going out in public, it really can start to feel as if there's just no relief in reach.

Therapy, specifically cognitive behavioral therapy (CBT), can help us repattern our thinking and behavior in social situations through "exposure treatment." As *Harvard Health* points out, "In exposure therapy, . . . therapists gradually expose patients to the dreaded situation and suggest ways to manage fear. If an upcoming office party seems overwhelming, for example, one way to cope with it is to establish an achievable goal—such as striking up a conversation with one or two people."[4] Exposure therapy requires us to conclude that we don't want to suffer anymore and we're willing to do anything to achieve that goal. Once we make up our mind, the therapist can be there to help remind us why we made the decision and gently continue to walk us through the increasingly anxiety-provoking exposures, helping us to conquer them one by one. A therapist might even remind us of how successful this treatment can be, over and over again, as a means of helping us keep our eyes on the prize. According to *Harvard Health*, "One-half to two-thirds of patients who underwent CBT experienced clinically meaningful improvements in symptoms after 12 weeks of therapy."[5]

People who do not find success from CBT techniques may consider medication. Many of our mental health symptoms are caused by neurotransmitters that aren't functioning as they should. Reductions in serotonin, for example, well known for pushing us into depression, play a serious role when it comes to our experience of anxiety. In situations where our brain is the culprit behind our symptoms, medication could be the key to unlocking the suffering and finding healing.

As a reminder, there should never be any judgment about taking medication for depression, anxiety, or any other mental health symptom if we've been assessed to need those medications by a medical doctor to help restore our brain to normal functioning. We don't hear of people being shamed for or ashamed of taking medication for diabetes, hypertension, or other common physical health diagnoses. We need to get to a point where we don't hear shame levied at people taking medication for mental health diagnoses either.

What the Bible Says about Social Anxiety

> The LORD God said: It is not good for the man to be alone.
> —Genesis 2:18

God deeply understands our condition. He recognizes the struggles we face mentally and emotionally, and the Bible openly talks about all our deepest pain and suffering in clear and beautiful ways.

We are not meant to be alone. Instead, we were created to be a part of the Body of Christ, where every single member of the Body is as important as every other member. We need one another to navigate our dark valleys, to walk together toward God, and we need one another for health and happiness. Ultimately God is the only one who can satisfy our hearts, and one of the ways he most clearly comes to us is through others.

Our intense desire to isolate ourselves as a means of surviving our intense social anxiety only doubles down our pain and suffering. Decreasing support and social interaction with others in our communities leads to shame, depression, and a rebound of fear and anxiety that keeps us away if we don't confront it and push forward.

One of the roots of our social anxiety is getting stuck in a spiral of thoughts about what others might think of us and the judgments we think they're making about us. Scripture offers us an antidote to this kind of unhealthy thinking: "Keeping our eyes fixed on Jesus" (Heb 12:2). If we can remember what's truly important, we can avoid a whole lot of unnecessary anxiety and worry.

Our social anxiety can make us feel weak: *Why doesn't my faith power me through this anxiety? Do I not believe enough? Is God punishing me by allowing me to experience this anxiety because I've done something wrong? Doesn't God love me?*

St. Paul provides an answer: "He said to me, 'My grace is sufficient for you, for power is made perfect in weakness'" (2 Cor 12:9). There's something about our weakness, our struggles, and even our anxiety and panic that opens us up to the power of Christ. Christ didn't come for the strong; he came for the weak. And as St. Peter says in 1 Peter 5:7, "Cast all your worries upon him because he cares for you." Sure, this message doesn't resolve my anxiety, but it does remind me that my weakness doesn't mean there's something wrong with me, and it certainly doesn't mean that Christ isn't close to me. It's precisely the opposite. If we can keep our eyes focused on Christ, his grace will sustain us and come to us in more ways than we can imagine.

What the Saints Say about Social Anxiety

> We who run in the way of love shouldn't be thinking of sufferings that can take place in the future.
>
> —St. Thérèse of Lisieux

It can be easy to think that St. Thérèse of Lisieux had it all figured out. She knew that one of the best ways to battle our social anxiety is to focus on the present and not worry about the sufferings or embarrassments that might take place in the future. This is key, but it isn't easy—it wasn't easy for her either.

Marie Françoise-Thérèse Martin was born in 1873 in France to devout Catholic parents who had nine children in all. Most know her as St. Thérèse of Lisieux, the discalced Carmelite who would go on to be declared a Doctor of the Church despite dying at the age of twenty-four. Her "little way" has become a beloved spirituality and way to grow in holiness for countless Christians down through the ages.

While less well known, her mental health struggles in life also paint a picture of someone who suffered greatly. She lost her mother to death and a sister to the cloister at an early age and was completely changed by her grief. After the death of her mother, Thérèse wrote, "When Mummy died, my happy disposition changed. I had been so lively and open; now I became diffident and oversensitive, crying if anyone looked at me. I was only happy if no one took notice of me. . . . It was only in the intimacy of my own family, where everyone was wonderfully kind, that I could be more myself."[6]

Thérèse was bullied in school, and this led to her experiencing what many of us would consider social anxiety. In addition to this, Thérèse experienced nervous tremors, clenched her teeth to the point of being unable to speak, and when examined by a doctor, was found to "react to an emotional frustration with a neurotic attack."[7] She also experienced scruples, and once wrote of her suffering, "One would have to pass through this martyrdom to understand it well, and for me to express what I experienced for a year and a half would be impossible."[8] Yet she didn't allow her experiences at school or her physical ailments to hold her back from God's call, choosing to join her sister in the Carmelite cloister at age fifteen, where she lived the rest of her life in service despite her continued suffering.

It's vitally important for us to look into the entire lives of our holy heroes, to see their heroic virtue amid the deep suffering, pain, and mental anguish they experienced throughout their lives. When we look at our own suffering, anxiety, or fear and panic, it can start to feel like we don't really have a chance to become a saint or to even make meaningful gains in our striving to become holy. And yet saints such as Thérèse show us just how much of a lie that message is.

Jesus is there, ready for us to collapse into his open arms, no matter if we've conquered our anxiety or have been conquered by it. As St. Edith Stein, Teresa Benedicta of the Cross, reminds us, "And when night comes, and you look back over your day and see . . . all the reasons you have to be embarrassed and ashamed: just take everything exactly as it is, put it in God's hands, and leave it with Him." Handing it all over to him takes effort and practice, but if we pray for the grace to be able to do it, we will feel less burdened.

IN BRIEF

- Social anxiety disorder is an intense, persistent fear of being watched and judged by others.
- Social anxiety is not just being an introvert; it's a serious mental health issue that requires intervention in order to live the life of peace.
- When the thing we're afraid of is being around other people, staying away leads to consequences in many aspects of our lives.
- Avoiding anxiety-provoking situations by leaving home only at times that feel safe isn't a healthy solution to social anxiety. Instead, we

must walk into the hurricane—sometimes in the form of exposure therapy.

- Sometimes facing our fears is going out in the social situations that cause us anxiety; sometimes that means first getting treatment, such as cognitive behavioral therapy or medication.

CLOSING PRAYER

And of what should we be afraid? Our captain on this battlefield is Christ Jesus. We have discovered what we have to do. Christ has bound our enemies for us and weakened them that they cannot overcome us unless we so choose to let them. So we must fight courageously and mark ourselves with the sign of the most Holy Cross.

—St. Catherine of Siena

7. OBSESSIVE-COMPULSIVE DISORDER

LORD, THE ONE YOU LOVE IS BATTLING INTRUSIVE THOUGHTS

Intrusive thoughts are one of the most commonly shared human experiences and one of our most closely guarded secrets. Daily, we have thoughts that pop into our head that scare us, make us question if we're a good person, and leave us feeling we'd do absolutely anything to keep those thoughts from assaulting us ever again.

Sometimes we're able to shrug off these thoughts with little more than a "What in the world was that?!" But sometimes these thoughts become intensely disturbing and end up taking control of our lives.

Obsessive-compulsive disorder (OCD) involves having intrusive thoughts pop into our mind without our consent, becoming overwhelmingly obsessed with those thoughts, and then desperately trying to alleviate the anxiety caused by those thoughts. The behaviors that we turn to for relief, control, and a sense of peace are called compulsions.

This cycle of obsessions and compulsions is anything but peaceful.

OCD Isn't Just Liking Things to Be Neat, Clean, and in Order

"I'm kind of OCD." How many times have we heard this statement from friends or coworkers? It's meant to signify that they like things organized, they like routine, and they feel stressed when things aren't in order. However, obsessive-compulsive disorder is so much more than liking things lined up, orderly, and put away. According to the American Psychiatric Association, OCD "is an anxiety disorder in which people have recurring unwanted thoughts, ideas, or sensations (obsessions) that make them feel driven to do something repetitively (compulsions). The repetitive behaviors, such as hand washing, checking on things, or cleaning, can significantly interfere with a person's daily activities and social interactions."[1]

More than just liking to be clean and washing our hands after we touch doorknobs in public, OCD paralyzes us with unwanted thoughts and drives us to engage in a behavior to the point that the behavior interferes with our ability to function in everyday life. It's less *I touched a doorknob that's maybe dirty, so I better wash my hands* and more *I touched a doorknob that's dirty and that means I could pick up a disease that I could bring home to my family and that disease might kill my child.* And then after washing our hands, we start to think, *I didn't do that quite right, I need to wash again*, and then, *I think my hand bumped the faucet, I need to wash again*, until it gets to the point where hand washing disrupts our ability to carry out our responsibilities.

Common obsessions include thoughts of contamination (germs, bodily fluids, etc.), unwanted sexual thoughts (forbidden or perverse images or sexual orientation), fear of losing control (impulsively acting in a way that could hurt ourselves or others), harm (being responsible for something tragic happening, such as running over someone with your car), perfectionism (needing things to be even or exact or worrying about if you can throw things away or not), and religious themes (which we will discuss in the next chapter).[2] Some of these obsessive and intrusive thoughts can be quite disturbing, and this leads those of us suffering from them to refrain from reaching out for help because we're worried about being judged. We can start to think that these intrusive thoughts say something about our moral character, and this crushes our self-esteem.

Compulsions develop in response to wanting these obsessive thoughts to go away or, at the very least, for the anxiety they cause to be minimized. We usually know that our compulsions aren't rational and they aren't going to prevent the thing we're worried about. We would much rather not engage in them, but we can't help ourselves.

Compulsions are borne from the obsessive thoughts. Common compulsions involve excessive cleaning (hand washing or cleaning around the home), checking (making sure we didn't run over someone with our car, checking the stove to make sure it's off), repeating (completing activities over and over again until they feel right), and thinking (counting, praying, or canceling a bad word by replacing it with a good word).[3] A compulsion goes beyond making sure the front door is locked one extra time before going to bed to repeatedly getting out of bed, not being able to sleep, because you have to check the lock.

So What Do We Do?

In order to effectively heal from OCD, with the help of a therapist, we need to slowly expose ourselves to the obsessive triggers and sit with our anxiety, preventing ourselves from engaging in the compulsive behaviors that bring us relief. If that sounds hard, it is. But it's also *really* effective.

The Anxiety and Depression Association of America provides us with an example of how therapy might play out:

> Let's say you have an obsessive fear of germs in public places, and that fear is pretty low in how much it scares you. Your therapist will design a task for you that exposes you to that fear. Your task might be for you to touch a public doorknob. . . . If your usual response is to wash your hands immediately after touching the doorknob, the therapist would ask you to wait before you wash your hands. As you repeat this exposure task, the therapist will ask you to wait longer and longer before washing your hands. Over time, this gradual exposure and delayed response would help you learn to control your fear of germs in public places without washing your hands.[4]

A precursor to this therapeutic technique, called exposure and response prevention (ERP), may be imagining a situation that brings us anxiety through visualization. A therapist may lead us through a guided experience in our mind, walking us through a situation that would bring us anxiety and worry. We imagine the situation and not responding to the desire to engage in compulsive behavior.

Eventually, by sitting through the anxiety and panic, we start to recognize nothing bad happens when we refrain from our compulsive behaviors, and the anxiety slowly starts to decrease. This is called habituation, and the more habituated we are, the less control the obsessive thoughts have over us.

Is There Healing and Relief Out There?

Living with OCD can be overwhelming, leaving us feeling hopeless. To compound matters, few therapists are experts in OCD, and a person could go in for treatment and be walked through interventions that could actually make OCD worse (such as confronting the intrusive thoughts and trying to come up with a more rational thought, for example, which is a typical intervention in cognitive behavioral therapy). Because of their scarcity, experts in OCD treatment can be pricey, creating a cost barrier for most of us. Add to that the fact that exposure and response prevention doesn't sound all that appealing, and you've got the perfect storm for those suffering from OCD to continue suffering for years.

But research shows that ERP is a highly successful treatment: about two-thirds of ERP patients experience improvement in symptoms, and about one-third of patients are considered recovered.[5] If people can find it and get access to it, they can be relatively positive about their wellness and recovery. There are a good number of workbooks available that will help guide us through the ERP process.[6] When ERP isn't available or effective, medication may help. Begin by talking to your primary care physician.

What the Bible Says about OCD

> It is not that I have already taken hold of it or have already attained perfect maturity, but I continue my pursuit in hope that I may possess it, since I have indeed been taken possession of by Christ.
>
> —Philippians 3:12

One of the biggest issues with OCD for those of us striving to live a life of holiness is the idea that our intrusive thoughts are telling us something about who we are. We experience intrusive thoughts about immorality, and we start to worry that they expose some deep truth about the horrible person we are.

This couldn't be further from the truth. No matter what intrusive thoughts come into our head, assaulting us without our wanting them to be there, God sees it, knows what it is, and does not condemn us or think any less of us for it. "Know the God of your father and serve him with a whole heart and a willing soul, for the Lord searches all hearts and understands all the mind's thoughts" (1 Chr 28:9).

Those of us undergoing ERP will also find strength in Proverbs: "The patient are better than warriors, and those who rule their temper, better than the conqueror of a city" (Prv16:32). To fight against OCD, to take control over our thoughts and behaviors, we must be patient, we must sit in the hurricane of anxiety and stand strong, and we must face our fears and conquer them. And when we're able to do that, after a whole lot of failure and trying again, we will stand tall, stronger than "the conqueror of a city."

In our weakness, we have an opportunity to show God's strength, God's glory, and God's love working in our lives. We do this with patience and perseverance, by continuing to put one foot in front of the other even when it's hard.

What the Saints Say about OCD

> We cannot do everything, and there is a sense of liberation in realizing that. This enables us to do something, and to do it very well. It may be incomplete, but it is a beginning, a step along the way, an opportunity for the Lord's grace to enter and do the rest.
>
> —St. Óscar Romero

When we look at the anxiety and compulsive behavior related to OCD, would you believe we have a friend in St. Óscar Romero?

Born in 1917 in El Salvador, Romero, one of eight children, entered the minor seminary at the age of thirteen. He was ordained a priest in

1942, appointed an auxiliary bishop in 1970, and became bishop of San Salvador seven years later. The government was pleased with his appointment, while many priests in the area were disappointed. He had a conservative reputation and was not well known for speaking out on behalf of the poor and suffering.

Then on March 12, 1977, everything changed.

Fr. Rutilio Grande, a Jesuit priest and Romero's good friend, was assassinated. The impact of this event on Romero would change the course of his life. He said of the incident, "When I looked at Rutilio lying there dead, I thought, 'If they have killed him for doing what he did, then I too have to walk the same path.'"[7]

From that moment on, Romero became a champion of the poor and the oppressed and would routinely speak out against injustice, violence, and sin. This would eventually lead to Romero's own assassination; while celebrating Mass on March 24, 1980, after giving his homily, he was shot in the heart by a gunman.

The story of his life has inspired countless Catholics through the years, but one piece that often gets left out is that he was diagnosed with obsessive-compulsive personality disorder. As journalist Peter Jesserer Smith explains, Romero's OCD symptoms eventual led him to suffer a nervous breakdown, but "Blessed Romero . . . eventually decided to seek psychoanalysis and long-term therapy, which deepened his personal intimacy with God."[8]

Too often, the stigma associated with therapy, especially in religious circles, keeps people away from getting help and leads to unnecessary suffering. The life of St. Óscar Romero pushes back against that stigma.

May we feel empowered to reach out to St. Óscar Romero when we feel overwhelmed by obsessive-compulsive thoughts, desperate to grasp at any way to control our lives, and may he lead us closer to Christ and one another.

IN BRIEF

- OCD is being paralyzed by unwanted thoughts and driven to engage in behaviors to the point that they interfere with our ability to function in everyday life.
- Obsessions are recurrent and persistent thoughts, impulses, or images that cause distressing emotions such as anxiety or disgust. Many of us with OCD recognize that the thoughts, impulses, or images are products of our mind and are excessive or unreasonable. Yet these intrusive thoughts cannot be settled by logic or reasoning.
- Compulsions are repetitive behaviors or mental acts that we feel driven to perform in response to obsessions. The behaviors are aimed at preventing or reducing distress or feared situations. In the most severe cases, a constant repetition of rituals may fill the day, making a normal routine impossible.
- In exposure and response prevention, a therapist may lead us through a guided experience in our mind, walking us through the situation that would bring us anxiety and worry and not responding to the desire to engage in compulsive behavior.

CLOSING PRAYER

Go forth in peace, for you have followed the good road. Go forth without fear, for he who created you has made you holy, has always protected you, and loves you as a mother. Blessed be you, my God, for having created me.

—St. Clare of Assisi

8. SCRUPULOSITY

LORD, THE ONE YOU LOVE HAS RELIGIOUS OCD

Shortly after my wife and I had our first child, we had a reversion to our Catholic faith and grew deeper in our desire to follow the teaching of Christ and his Church. This reversion led me to complete an examination of conscience, and I knew that I was engaged in one particular sin that I had to take to Confession as we started down this path. It wasn't an easy sin for me to want to bring up in Confession, but I knew I needed to.

When I finally mustered the courage to go into Confession and lay it all out on the line, my scrupulous heart did not find comfort and relief but rather was met with anxiety, panic, and a continued feeling of not being good enough for God to love me. The priest I met with replied to the confession of my sin by making an excuse for my behavior, saying, "That's not actually a sin, despite what you've been told."

I was mortified.

What was going to happen to me? Was my absolution efficacious? Did I need to go again, pray an act of contrition, or just give up everything and live a life of penance and prayer in the nearest monastery? I felt robbed of a clear answer, and it weighed me down and filled me with an overwhelming anxiety.

I realize the Church has answers to all these questions; *trust me*, I looked them up in an attempt to assuage my anxieties. But reading the answers to those questions didn't help. While I could understand intellectually what they were saying and that they had truth behind them, I just wasn't feeling it in my heart.

And so, even though I didn't need to for this specific sin, I went back to Confession, to a different priest, and received a completely different reaction. This priest took my sin seriously, gave me a penance that I felt fitting, and as soon as I finished that penance, I finally felt that weight lifted off of my shoulders.

It wouldn't be long before I was overcome by the same feeling of committing a sin that wasn't forgiven, and this is a common experience for a lot of us trying our best to live a good life in the Catholic Church. It's called religious obsessive-compulsive disorder, or scrupulosity, and it's a serious struggle for more of us than you might realize.

Scrupulosity Isn't Just Being Focused on Holiness

People tend to write off the seriousness of scrupulosity by thinking that it simply means being focused on sin and wanting to be holy. However, according to the International OCD Foundation, scrupulosity is considered "a form of obsessive-compulsive disorder (OCD) involving religious or moral obsessions. Scrupulous individuals are overly concerned that something they thought or did might be a sin or other violation of religious or moral doctrine."[1] People who experience scrupulosity tend to obsess over things such as blasphemy, sin, and moral behavior, which results in behaviors such as excessive trips to Confession or to receive assurance from religious leaders, as well as acts of self-sacrifice.[2]

What makes these behaviors a mental health issue is that "unlike normal religious practice, scrupulous behavior usually exceeds or disregards religious law and may focus excessively on one trivial area of religious practice while other, more important areas may be completely ignored. The behavior of scrupulous individuals is typically inconsistent with that of the rest of the faith community."[3]

For those of us suffering from scrupulosity, we push aside the answers to our questions that should satisfy our hearts and put us at peace and remain buried in doubts. We focus ourselves on God's justice and ignore God's mercy. But we aren't doing these things with full consent of our will. Religious OCD hijacks our brain, fights against our rational thought process, and makes us do things or focus on things that we otherwise wouldn't choose to do or focus on.

So What Do We Do?

Coping with our scrupulosity lies in accepting and living in a world where nothing is for sure and realizing that we can't be harmed by that uncertainty. We might begin by focusing on these types of thoughts:

- Faith is not the absence of feeling uncertain. Faith is going forward through the uncertainty.
- OCD wants me to believe that uncertainty and doubt are dangerous. While uncertainty is uncomfortable, it is not dangerous, and I can tolerate it.
- My faith is what I believe, not what I feel.[4]

Feelings don't change the truth, but they do impact our ability to receive the truth and live in it. When it comes to scrupulosity, this fact is an important piece to our coping.

A large part of scrupulosity is the intrusive thoughts that can come into our mind and plague us to the point of being paralyzed with fear. We can deal with them by acknowledging them and recognizing that they don't mean we are a bad person or bad Christian. Doing this allows us to get a handle on these thoughts and keeps them from paralyzing us.

Our goal is to "starve" our scrupulosity by not giving meaning to the thoughts that we're having. This approach obviously takes practice; it doesn't work right away because it isn't a natural reaction to the situation. When we think, *I'm going to hell because of my sinful thoughts*, our natural reaction is to figure out a way to disprove the idea. However, this attention and effort actually feeds our scrupulous thoughts, making them more likely to come back and to do so with a vengeance. Instead, we should feel the thought and then say, *Well that's just my scrupulosity, that's just my OCD*. By labeling it and moving forward, the thoughts begin to lose their power over us, and over time, they will decrease in their frequency and intensity.

Is There Healing and Relief Out There?

Treatment for scrupulosity is often the same treatment used with other forms of OCD, including cognitive behavior therapy, and specifically exposure and response prevention (ERP).[5]

Some examples of ERP interventions for scrupulosity, which increase in risk level with time, might include

- sampling a piece of cheese at a deli then walking away, stimulating the idea of stealing,
- taking a piece of paper and then littering on the street, or
- repeating to yourself that the Virgin Mary may not have really been a virgin.[6]

Some of these things feel downright wrong to do even for the purposes of therapeutic treatment, and unfortunately this keeps a lot of people from engaging in ERP for scrupulosity. However, it's important to remember that these are simply exercises for the sake of learning to better cope with the symptoms of religious OCD; they are not willfully committed as sins. As marriage and family therapist Kevin Foss explains, "Part of ERP is making space in your mind for uncomfortable, controversial, or taboo thoughts instead of fighting to suppress them. Doing so will not slowly erode your moral character or flip you 180 degrees into a world-class sinner. It is not a virus that will infect you upon contact. Instead, you will learn that you can gently allow for the thought and feeling to visit you for a period of time and then move on, and it won't take you with it."[7]

ERP can help us take away the power of these thoughts, remove their power over us, and help us finally break free in our lives to live in God's love, mercy, and peace.

Medication might also be an avenue where those of us suffering from scrupulosity might find healing.

Whether your path is to find healing through therapy, medication, or both, the time to start down that path is now. Many of us who suffer from scrupulosity wait years before seeking help from a mental health professional. God wants us to experience his peace, mercy, and consolation, and he's waiting to provide that to us through those very same mental health professionals.

What the Bible Says about Scrupulosity

> For by grace you have been saved through faith, and this is not from you; it is the gift of God; it is not from works, so no one may boast.
>
> —Ephesians 2:8–9

Jesus saves us, and God brings us to heaven. When we are considering scrupulosity, I find it important to lean into the truth that faith and salvation are gifts from God that are not earned by any of us. Of course, we have to respond to those gifts and cooperate with his grace, but when we're stuck in the endless shame cycle of scrupulosity, we typically focus on how we're "not good enough," "not doing enough," or "just not worthy of God's love and salvation."

All of that is true, and yet God *still* loves us, still wants us to be with him, and still decided to come down from heaven and take it all to the Cross for our sake. That's the message of Christianity, and that's the message that gets so easily lost when we experience scrupulosity.

1 Thessalonians 5:24 really drives this point home: "The one who calls you is faithful, and he will also accomplish it." When we're battling scrupulosity, we have no choice but to turn to him and trust he will do as he says, even though our hearts aren't feeling it.

That's the freeing power waiting for us in Christianity. If only experiencing it as a feeling in our hearts was as easy as understanding it as a fact in our minds! Those of us experiencing scrupulosity know that it isn't. And so we wait. We try to work through the symptoms, and we wait for our hearts to feel it again. Like the psalmist, we cry out: "Since my heart was embittered and my soul deeply wounded, I was stupid and could not understand; I was like a brute beast in your presence." But we also keep our heads held high as we finish the verse: "Yet I am always with you; you take hold of my right hand" (Ps 73:21–23).

What the Saints Say about Scrupulosity

> Despite my repentance, I thought: I am still consecrated to Satan, and I am still his slave and property as he awaits me in Hell. As I pondered over my condition, I experienced a deep sense of despair and almost committed suicide.
>
> —Bl. Bartolo Longo

Bl. Bartolo Longo was born into a wealthy family in Italy in 1841. His father died when Bartolo was just ten years old. While in college studying to become a lawyer, Bartolo became connected to a group that was involved in witchcraft and occultism. This eventually led to him not only joining a satanic cult but also being ordained as a satanic priest.

His mental health began to suffer as a result of this wrong path he had chosen. He started to experience depression, anxiety, difficulty concentrating, and even paranoia. Suffering, he went to visit an old friend and ask for advice. His friend responded in a way that cut Bartolo to the heart, noting that if he continued down this path, it would lead to complete and utter madness.[8]

This set Bartolo off on a journey toward a complete reversion to the Catholic faith. He even attended a séance and held up a miraculous medal while declaring, "I renounce spiritualism because it is nothing but a maze of error and falsehood," as a sign of leaving behind his old ways.[9]

However, even Bartolo's complete and total 180-degree conversion wasn't enough to chase off scrupulosity. He still worried that his repentance wasn't enough, that he was still consecrated to Satan.

Understanding that our holy heroes struggled even after they understood their mission in life can help us not only to relate to them but also to cope with our anxiety as we struggle to figure out how to leave behind our scrupulosity and grow in holiness. Those who are in heaven right this very moment struggled to rest comfortably in the promises of God, which can give us hope, confidence, and peace.

IN BRIEF

- Scrupulosity is a form of obsessive-compulsive disorder (OCD) involving religious or moral obsessions. Scrupulous individuals are overly concerned that something they thought or did might be a sin or other violation of religious or moral doctrine.
- Unlike normal religious practice, scrupulous behavior usually exceeds or disregards religious law and may focus excessively on one trivial area of religious practice, while other, more important areas may be completely ignored. The behavior of scrupulous individuals is typically inconsistent with that of the rest of the faith community.
- Having faith doesn't mean we're just blissful about every difficult situation that pops up in our lives but rather that we accept the trials and questions we're facing and keep moving forward. Living in this uncertainty is the key. At the same time, we have to recognize that it's really, really hard.
- The goal is to "starve" our scrupulosity by not giving meaning to the intrusive, scrupulous thoughts that we're having. Labeling a scrupulous thought as exactly that and then letting it exist without giving it too much attention is one of the best things we can do.
- Don't put off therapy, medication, or both. Many of us who suffer from scrupulosity wait years before seeking help from mental health professionals, and we don't deserve all that suffering. God wants us to experience his peace, mercy, and consolation, and he's waiting to provide that to us through those very same mental health professionals.

CLOSING PRAYER

Receive, O Lord, all my liberty. Take my memory, my understanding, and my entire will. Whatsoever I have or hold, Thou hast given me; I give it all back to Thee and commit it wholly to be governed by Thy will. Thy love and Thy grace give unto me, and I am rich enough and ask for nothing more.

—St. Ignatius of Loyola

TRAUMA

9. POST-TRAUMATIC STRESS DISORDER

LORD, THE ONE YOU LOVE FEELS HELPLESS

If you've taken any psychology classes, you most likely covered learned helplessness and experiments done by Martin Seligman and his colleagues in the mid-1960s, in which they would ring a bell and then give a light shock to a dog. Eventually the dog would react to the sound of the bell as if he had been shocked. Seligman later put the dog in a large crate that was divided in two by a low fence the dog could jump over and electrified on one side. Instead of jumping over the fence to get away from the shock and the electrified side, the dog lay down, as if he had learned there was nothing he could do to escape the shocks and so he wouldn't try.[1]

It's easy to see how this lesson can apply to our human experience after living through traumatic events. When we've been through trauma, we can develop this feeling of helplessness, that there's no way to escape our trauma so we might as well just lie down and let it wash over us.

This also shows why we're so reluctant to reach out for help with the symptoms that develop after we've faced trauma, such as flashbacks, numbness, avoidance, hypervigilance, jumpiness, and decreased ability to tolerate frustration. Our brain can learn to feel helpless just like the dog in the Seligman experiment. We can feel stuck, like nothing will ever stop our pain. Or even worse, we can feel guilty because of our experience and start to think we somehow deserve the fallout.

PTSD Isn't Just Experienced by People Who Survived a Combat Zone

Of all the mental health experiences we can go through, post-traumatic stress disorder is one of the most difficult and sadly one that seems to be becoming more common—around eight million adults experience diagnosable post-traumatic stress disorder (PTSD) during any given year.[2] While feeling afraid and panicked in the middle of a stressful or traumatic situation is normal, PTSD comes into play when these feelings or reactions continue to persist in us long after the traumatic event has occurred. These symptoms can be so intense and pervasive that they begin to impact our ability to function in our everyday lives.

We most often think of PTSD as being something war veterans experience. However, people can suffer from this after any trauma they experience. For an adult to be diagnosed with PTSD, they must experience in at least one month

- one or more reexperiencing symptoms (flashbacks, bad dreams, or frightening thoughts borne out of the traumatic event);
- one or more avoidance symptoms (avoiding places, events, thoughts, or feelings related to the traumatic event);
- two or more arousal or reactivity symptoms (easily startled, tension, sleeping difficulties, or angry outbursts); and
- two or more cognition or mood symptoms (difficulty remembering details related to the traumatic event, negative feelings, disproportionate feelings of guilt or blame, or loss of interest in activities).[3]

PTSD is a pervasive experience that impacts many different facets of our lives. Because of this all-encompassing suffering, we can see clearly how hopelessness can start to creep into our minds. We were the victim of a traumatic experience, peace was ripped away from us, and how can we ever reclaim what was stolen? Or we think that the trauma we experienced wasn't "traumatic enough" compared to what other people have experienced, so we shouldn't complain. Because of those thoughts, we can tend to stay away from reaching out for help, from therapy and/or medication, and just throw up our hands and feel as if we're destined to continue suffering. However, by not getting help we fall into the vicious spiral of learned helplessness, when our growing feelings of anxiety and depression caused by untreated trauma increase our sense of helplessness. And that's why we've got to step in and do something about it!

So What Do We Do?

The first thing we have to do is realize that we aren't helpless! This involves restructuring our thoughts to help us come to a more rational understanding of our situation. We need to acknowledge our feelings of helplessness and then ask ourselves, *What evidence is there to support these feelings versus the evidence to support the idea that I'm not helpless?*

Feeling depressed, anxious, or panicked doesn't necessarily mean that we're helpless. Have we looked into various ways of coping and then tried them? Can we examine potential coping skills we haven't tried and maybe rank them in terms of what we're most willing to try first?

We're going to explore three coping skills before we explore what help might be out there beyond what we can do for ourselves.[4]

Exercise

Even the smallest amount of exercise can have a huge impact on our mental health and especially on symptoms related to traumatic events, mostly because it's not something that's directly related to our symptoms. It's not some therapeutic technique we'd find in a workbook, so we're less likely to reject it with thoughts like, *Well, this isn't going to work*, precisely because it doesn't feel like a therapy at all.

Reach Out

Our brain is telling us that isolation is the best path to reducing our anxiety, especially when we're feeling helpless. But it's a lie. The more we turn inward on ourselves, the less likely we'll find recovery and healing *even when we're engaging in other coping skills*. We have to keep reminding ourselves of this as we reach out to others, whether it be for casual chatting and activities or deeper conversation.

Find Calm

We have the ability to take control of our mind and our body, even when we're feeling out of control. Breathing exercises, mindfulness exercises, and grounding exercises all help us get out of our spiraling mind and into the present moment so we can ditch the anxiety.

As with many other mental health experiences, we also have to learn to accept that sometimes we will be assaulted by feelings related to the trauma we experienced and have to ride them out. We need to work on recognizing those feelings, accepting that they've come into our mind without our consent; acknowledge that they are causing us stress and anxiety; and ride out the experience with the aforementioned self-regulating techniques. Overcoming the overwhelming feeling of helplessness isn't easy, but it is possible.

Is There Healing and Relief Out There?

PTSD is difficult to overcome, but there's hope. According to the health writer Wyatt Myers, "More recently doctors have had great success treating and healing those with the stress and anxiety related to PTSD. The key is getting the right kind of treatment. PTSD is not a condition that will resolve on its own."[5]

Something has to be done to help us move toward recovery when we're experiencing PTSD. For some of us, that may mean learning coping skills that we can do on our own. For others, that may mean engaging one of the various types of therapy that help people find freedom from helplessness. And for others, medication might be necessary to help fight off feelings of helplessness.

Cognitive processing therapy (CPT) is a method of therapy that helps us learn how to work on our upsetting thoughts and try to change those thoughts to hopefully help alleviate our negative feelings.

Based in cognitive behavioral therapy, CPT helps us develop more rational and fact-based thoughts by guiding us to examine thoughts we have about our trauma, our helplessness, and even the way the world works in general. Once we look at the thoughts causing us problems—self-blaming thoughts, for example—we start to modify those thoughts, replace them with ones that are more fact based, and experience relief from our symptoms.

Eye movement desensitization and reprocessing (EMDR) is another therapeutic treatment for PTSD. The method uses eye movements to help process memories one at a time, as the clinician "asks the client to hold different aspects of that event or thought in mind and to use his eyes to track the therapist's hand as it moves back and forth across the client's field of vision. As this happens, for reasons believed by a Harvard researcher to be connected with the biological mechanisms involved in Rapid Eye Movement (REM) sleep, internal associations arise and the client begins to process the memory and disturbing feelings. In successful EMDR therapy, the meaning of painful events is transformed on an emotional level."[6]

Therapists certified in EMDR can be difficult to find and often pricey. And while many people have found healing and wellness through EMDR treatment, it's not without controversy. Francine Shapiro, the developer of this treatment, has been called out for increasing the length and expense of the training and certification that she requires clinicians to complete; and she allegedly does this whenever a study comes out that presents a less-than-perfect result from her treatment modality.[7] In addition, a study done in 2000 put forth the idea that the theory leading to the development of EMDR was not falsifiable and therefore not something that could be studied scientifically.[8]

All that being said, EMDR has changed many people's lives after trauma. Perhaps the best takeaway here is to think about our personality, preferred methods for learning, and what we think about mental health and recovery from mental health symptoms and then seek out the therapeutic method that best aligns with who we are.

What the Bible Says about Helplessness

> For I know well the plans I have in mind for you . . . plans for your welfare and not for woe, so as to give you a future of hope. When you call me, and come and pray to me, I will listen to you. When you look for me, you will find me. Yes, when you seek me with all your heart, I will let you find me.
>
> —Jeremiah 29:11–14

Feeling helpless seems to be a part of human nature, especially because we're often trying to control things, and it's inevitable there will be some things that we can't control, that overwhelm us. But we aren't alone.

One of the central themes in our Christian faith is that even when we feel helpless, even when we don't see a way out, Christ is there with us. As St. Paul said, "For Christ, while we were still helpless, yet died at the appointed time" (Rom 5:6). God doesn't expect us to figure everything out on our own; he doesn't come to us thinking he's going to find us healthy, well, and on the right track. He knows we're broken, lost, and feeling helpless.

But he comes anyway.

He comes into our hearts to bring us the grace we need to turn to him when we're suffering. He comes into our lives through our loved ones, friends, and community to help us along the path of healing and wellness when we can't do it on our own and don't know how to take the first step.

It's so easy for us to feel like Job when we're suffering through an experience of helplessness: "Have I no helper, and has my good sense deserted me?" (Jb 6:13). But thankfully, we have a helper, an advocate, and people in our lives who can help us, whether loved ones or helping professionals.

And we have God, who tells us, "Do not fear: I am with you; do not be anxious: I am your God. I will strengthen you, I will help you, I will uphold you with my victorious right hand" (Is 41:10). Even when we feel helpless, even when past experiences overwhelm us, God is with us.

What the Saints Say about Helplessness

> A cheerful attitude will sustain you in all your difficulties, trials and sufferings in life.
>
> —Bl. Laura Vicuña

When I've been going through difficulties, it's been easy for me to see God as an all-powerful being, far removed from my situation, who has never felt helpless, little, or broken. And yet as the Venerable Fulton J. Sheen reminds us, "Divinity came to earthly life in the form of a helpless Babe, and left it in the form of a helpless Man."[9] These words help me see that there is something about suffering, about that experience of feeling helpless, that draws us into the heart of Christ. It's the place we find him, and in that place we can find the power and victory that seems so far out of our reach in the present moment.

Bl. Laura Vicuña would agree. Laura del Carmen Vicuña was born in 1891 in Santiago, Chile. Her parents were aristocrats, and their family was pushed out of their home after a revolution swept the country. After the death of her father, Laura's mother moved the family to be with her sisters in Argentina, where she took a job at a local hostel to help pay for Laura's education.

Laura was mocked by her classmates for delving so deeply into her Catholic faith. On two separate occasions she was beaten by the man in an abusive relationship with her mother who was paying for her education, because of her desire to become a religious sister. She pushed on, and her dedication was so inspiring that the religious sisters gave her a scholarship to attend school after this man decided to stop paying. Despite her joy in still being able to attend school, Laura was sad over the abuse and difficulties her mother was going through, and she made the decision to give her life for her mother: "Before she died, Laura told her mother: 'Mama, I offer my life for you, I asked our Lord for this. Before I die, Mother, would I have the joy of seeing you repent?' Mercedes crying, answered: 'I swear, I will do whatever you ask me! God is the witness of my promise!' Laura smiled and said: 'Thank you, Jesus! Thank you, Mary! Goodbye, Mother! Now I die happy!'"[10]

Laura died of tuberculosis on January 22, 1904.

The bravery of this girl, in the face of being torn away from her home and normal life, the death of her father and the grief that followed, and the abuse she suffered and watched her mother suffer, only to offer up her life for her mother in a way like this? Her story encourages us to ask for her intercession when we're feeling helpless, lost, broken, and don't know where else to turn. She's surely ready and waiting to pray for us and ask Jesus to give us his peace and consolation.

IN BRIEF

- Of all the various mental health experiences we can go through, post-traumatic stress disorder is one of the most difficult, and sadly one that seems to be becoming more and more common.
- Breathing exercises, mindfulness exercises, and grounding exercises can help us get out of our spiraling mind and into the present moment so we can ditch the anxiety.
- Sometimes we're going to be assaulted by feelings and have to ride them out. To do this, we recognize those feelings, accept that they've come into our mind without our consent, acknowledge that they are causing us stress and anxiety, and implement self-regulating techniques such as exercise, socializing, and calming practices until those feelings subside.
- Cognitive processing therapy and eye movement desensitization and reprocessing are forms of therapy that can help us move forward through life after trauma.

CLOSING PRAYER

> O Christ Jesus, when all is darkness and we feel our weakness and helplessness, give us the sense of your presence, your love, and your strength. Help us to have perfect trust in your protecting love and strengthening power, so that nothing may frighten or worry us, for, living close to you, we shall see your hand, your purpose, your will through all things.
>
> —St. Ignatius of Loyola

10. DISSOCIATION

LORD, THE ONE YOU LOVE IS FEELING DETACHED

We drove home from the hospital in a thick silence. We had just held our son in our arms and gave him all the love we could while we watched his little life slip away until he was gone.

Our brain has a few ways of protecting us when we're at risk of going into shock because a situation is too traumatic for us to comprehend. One of those is detaching us from the present reality, a mental health symptom often referred to as dissociation. When I look back on the birth of our son and the time before his death, I recognize that while I was present in the moment, I also felt outside of myself, as if I were watching the entire situation play out like a movie. As we drove home from the hospital, I was in a dreamlike state that made the real world feel foggy. My brain took me a step back from the situation to keep me from being paralyzed from the trauma.

Sometimes dissociation can continue to manifest even when we're safe and no longer in the midst of a traumatic event. We can find ourselves temporarily plucked out of reality as we try to function in our day-to-day lives, losing focus on what's going on around us. We can go on autopilot without even realizing it. We never know if this residue from our past trauma could interfere with what we are trying to accomplish, so not only does this symptom have the potential to make life nearly impossible but also there is fear and anxiety that the symptom will manifest.

It's all so paralyzing.

Dissociation Isn't Just Having a Hard Time Focusing

We've all had days where we have something on our mind that takes our focus away from the task at hand, leaving us stuck in our mind and maybe even losing track of time. But for most of us, we're able to shake it off and regain our focus. It's usually not something that happens day after day, week after week, month after month. And it's something we worry about happening when we least expect it.

In the case of living life after trauma, however, these experiences can be much more intense and complicated. As Dr. Matthew Tull, a professor of psychology at the University of Toledo and an expert in PTSD, explains, "Dissociation is a disconnection between a person's sensory experience, thoughts, sense of self, or personal history. People may feel a sense of unreality and lose their connection to time, place, and identity."[1]

Dissociation can be mild—feeling as if we're in a dream and not actually involved in the present moment, or feeling a persistent detachment from our lives, loved ones, friends, work, and even ourselves. Dissociation can also be severe—feeling as if we're breaking away from our identity, being completely absorbed in a flashback, losing memory, blanking out, or even feeling as if the world isn't real. We can also experience depersonalization, which involves out-of-body experiences that allow us to feel as if the event is not actually happening to us, and derealization, which involves experiencing events that aren't actually occurring.

Not knowing what may trigger an episode of dissociation can leave us, feeling paralyzed out of fear that we may become detached and lose the ability to safely navigate the world.

So What Do We Do?

Traumatic events change our understanding of the world and our thoughts about how relationships work. These changes can leave us experiencing all kinds of unwanted symptoms many years later. When we're ready to move forward and experience healing, we need to work through the impact of our trauma and develop a healthier outlook on relationships and life in general than our outlook influenced by our trauma. We try to recognize the impact that these symptoms are having on our lives and draw lines in our experience to help us know what exactly we're going through and why. We can start to do this by

- observing our patterns of dissociation and learning to tolerate the negative events and emotions that help trigger dissociation;
- accepting and loving ourselves, including the defenses that come from our trauma experiences;
- recognizing that the traumatic event happened and the impact of dissociation caused by it on our lives and relationships; and
- realizing that our increased awareness of our dissociation and its triggers brings us increased choices.[2]

Many of these steps and interventions can begin at home. While there is an obvious value to working with a professional, it's important to start where we can and take the small steps available to us in the moment to move forward toward health and well-being.

Observing our patterns of symptoms is a practice not only for the detachment common in PTSD but also for any of our mental health experiences. It gives us data from which we can start to have an honest assessment of our experience and share with a helping professional once we engage in treatment. In terms of detachment and dissociation, observing our patterns helps us identify how often we're experiencing the symptoms and see threads in our experience that might give us insight into why it's happening, what's causing it, and what we can do to cope in the healthiest ways possible.

When we're experiencing symptoms of dissociation after trauma, it's easy to criticize ourselves for not coping better. No one chooses to experience symptoms of detachment and dissociation, and yet we still berate ourselves for not successfully fending them off. If we want to find peace and healing, we've got to accept ourselves and our defenses, and realize that we're doing the best we can with everything that has happened. This acceptance and this choice to love ourselves in spite of our reaction to our trauma experience is a huge step forward toward finding that peace we deserve.

When we're more aware of and accepting of how we're responding to our experiences, we have more choices. It can be terrifying to fully engage in an experience that scares us to the point of wanting to avoid everything that might trigger another episode. But with increased awareness, we gain strength to work on wellness, have healthy relationships built on trust, and move forward after the experience of trauma.

Is There Healing and Relief Out There?

Coping with symptoms of dissociation includes grounding, a strategy that helps us to firmly plant ourselves in the present moment. When we start to feel dissociation coming on, we ground ourselves by asking, *Where am I? What am I doing right this minute?* Using our senses can also help bring us back into the present, similar to the coping skills we talked about earlier in relation to anxiety. We ask ourselves, *How many blue items can you see? What are five things I can smell right now?* These techniques help focus our mind on what is happening to us in the present moment rather than allowing our mind to be carried off because of whatever triggering thing happened.

We can also take a simple action to help engage our senses and ground us: chewing gum, holding ice cubes, or rubbing a scented lotion on our hands. Even something as simple as getting up and moving around to help get our heart pumping can help keep us from heading down the path of detachment.

In addition to coping skills we may pick up in therapy, we may also need to explore with our doctor potential medications that can help with symptoms of dissociation. While there are no medications specific to dissociative disorders, medication that can treat the mental health symptoms common to dissociative disorders can help mitigate the impact of the disorder.[3]

Whether our journey to healing and wellness from dissociation and detachment caused by PTSD involves working on things at home, engaging in individual therapy, or working with our doctor to find medication that brings us relief, it's important to know that there is healing, hope, and peaceful living in the present moment. It's there for all of us, and God wants us to find it along our journey to him.

What the Bible Says about Feeling Detached

> But whoever obeys me dwells in security, in peace, without fear of harm.
>
> —Proverbs 1:33

God knows we're anxious, loves us anyway, and wants us to experience peace. He wants us to have security and safety, to be free from harm. And while traumatic events may disrupt our sense of security, God holds our eternal safety and security in a way that can never be permanently taken from us. God is always present, even when it doesn't feel like it.

When we're anxious about what the new day might bring and paralyzed with fear over not knowing what might trigger symptoms of dissociation, we can remember that God goes before us, he's with us, and he will never forsake us. Yes, our symptoms, memories, and experiences will overwhelm us from time to time, but God is in control even in the moments where our lives feel the most out of control. He is our shelter. He guards us, and he wants to guide us to heaven so that we can be in the safety and security of his presence forever.

When we start to feel the oncoming symptoms of detachment or dissociation because of our past experience of trauma, we can repeat the words of Isaiah to ourselves as we prepare to engage in our grounding techniques to keep us in the present moment: "Do not fear: I am with you; do not be anxious: I am your God. I will strengthen you, I will help you, I will uphold you with my victorious right hand" (Is 41:10).

What the Saints Say about Feeling Detached

> When the grains of wheat are crushed and ground, wheat flour is obtained. We bake it to form the host for the Holy Eucharist. Similarly we too should be crushed in the mill of suffering and transformed to become like hosts.
>
> —St. Alphonsa Muttathupadathu

While few of our beloved holy heroes spoke directly on the experience of dissociation, many conveyed the pain of living after the experience of trauma and spoke to the importance of living in the present moment.

St. Gianna said, "Our task is to live holy the present moment." That task can be a struggle for most of us from time to time, especially when we're haunted by trauma and the symptoms of dissociation. But to be reminded that we only need to focus on what we can do in the present moment is freeing. We don't have to come up with big plans for the future; we don't have to worry about what symptoms we might experience when we're triggered. We only need to focus on what's happening now.

St. Alphonsa Muttathupadathu understood this well. Born in 1910, she experienced suffering from an early age. Her mother died when she was quite young, and she was raised by her abusive maternal aunt. When she was just three years old, she was diagnosed with a serious case of eczema that would torment her for more than a year after her diagnosis.

Shortly after starting school, Alphonsa (whose birth name was actually Anna) received a vision from St. Thérèse of Lisieux, one of her favorite saints, telling her that she was going to become a saint. After this vision, she decided that she wanted to dedicate her life to Christ. Her foster mother, however, had other plans and attempted to entice her to get married. In response to these attempts, Alphonsa fell into a pit of burning chaff, which burned her feet so badly that the idea of marriage was shelved, and she was permitted to join religious life.[4]

In 1931, she took her first vows as a religious sister, entering the part of her life where she would face her greatest trials and yet find her greatest strength. She became gravely ill with multiple different ailments. She was reportedly completely cured in 1936 through the intercession of St. Kuriakose Elias Chavara; however, her traumatic experiences were far from over:

> Painful illnesses followed each other: typhoid fever, double pneumonia, and, the most serious of all, a dramatic nervous shock, the result of a fright on seeing a thief during the night. . . . Her state of psychic incapacity lasted for about a year, during which she was unable to read or write. In every situation, Sister Alphonsa always maintained a great reservation and charitable attitude towards the Sisters, silently

> undergoing her sufferings. In 1945 she had a violent outbreak of illness. A tumor, which had spread throughout her organs, transformed her final year of life into a continuous agony. Gastroenteritis and liver problems caused violent convulsions and vomiting up to forty times a day: "I feel that the Lord has destined me to be an oblation, a sacrifice of suffering. . . . I consider a day in which I have not suffered as a day lost to me."[5]

She died with a smile on her lips on July 28, 1946, was beatified alongside Kuriakose Elias Chavara by Pope John Paul II forty years later, and was canonized by Pope Benedict XVI in 2008. Hundreds of inexplicable cures have been attributed to her intercession over the years.

We can ask for St. Alphonsa Muttathupadathu's intercession, in a life where we may have experienced unspeakable trauma, to ask our Lord to give us peace, consolation, and a heart like that of Sister Alphonsa, so that our sufferings can bring us transformation rather than keeping us trapped.

IN BRIEF

- Per Dr. Matthew Tull, "Dissociation is a disconnection between a person's sensory experience, thoughts, sense of self, or personal history. People may feel a sense of unreality and lose their connection to time, place, and identity."
- Not knowing what may trigger an episode of dissociation can leave us feeling paralyzed out of fear that we may become detached and lose the ability to safely navigate the world.
- Grounding is one way to cope with symptoms of dissociation. It is a strategy that helps us firmly plant ourselves in the present moment.
- If we work to increase our awareness, we work toward gaining strength to make choices for wellness and learn how to experience peace, have healthy relationships built on trust, and move forward after the experience of trauma.

CLOSING PRAYER

I believe, My God, that I am in Your presence, that You are looking at me and listening to my prayers. You are so great and so holy: I adore You. You have given me all: I thank You. You are so merciful: and I ask of You all the graces You know are beneficial to me. Amen.

—Bl. James Alberione

11. SELF-DESTRUCTIVENESS

LORD, THE ONE YOU LOVE IS HURTING THEMSELVES

Living a life marked by trauma is not easy. A single traumatic event can have repercussions for years, and the feelings associated with that trauma can be triggered unexpectedly and jump back into our otherwise peaceful world.

We can feel numb in the wake of intense trauma. Our body and brain check out, and we may feel it's better to feel nothing than to have to process the heart-shredding pain of what happened to us. Or we may search out something that will break through the numbness that surrounds us, something that can't be muted by the residue of our traumatic experience. This can involve various kinds of risky behavior—doing something dangerous but exhilarating. We may turn to substance abuse, thinking that drugs or excessive alcohol will aid us in finally feeling.

Or we may self-harm. While engaging in risky behavior or substance abuse are forms of self-harm, self-harm here refers to our engagement in behaviors that cause harm to our body—cutting, burning, hair pulling, and head banging, for example—as a means to help us cope.

Self-harm can be present in a whole host of mental health experiences, including depression, anxiety, dissociative disorders, and PTSD; it can even be found in those of us without any underlying mental health condition. Self-harm is prevalent in our society, and it isn't going to become less so until we learn to openly talk about our experiences and be willing to sit with those suffering from this without being scared away.

Self-Harm Is Not the Same Thing as Being Suicidal

"Self-harm is not a mental illness," the National Alliance on Mental Illness tells us, "but a behavior that indicates a need for better coping skills. . . . The urge to hurt yourself may start with overwhelming anger, frustration or pain. When a person is not sure how to deal with emotions, or learned as a child to hide emotions, self-harm may feel like a release. Sometimes, injuring yourself stimulates the body's endorphins or pain-killing hormones, thus raising their mood. Or if a person doesn't feel many emotions, they might cause themself pain in order to feel something 'real' to replace emotional numbness."[1]

Falling into a cycle of self-harm is a process. It develops after we've tried other coping skills to help with our situation, we still find ourselves suffering, and we're willing to do *anything* to feel peace and relief. Once we use self-harm to cope, the response to the behavior—a sense of relief from intense anxiety as the pain forces us out of our head, or simply feeling *something* that breaks our emotional numbness—reinforces the behavior in our mind.

A common misconception is that people engaging in self-harm are trying to kill themselves. Most of us who engage in self-harm, though, are actually trying to do something so we can continue living. "For some," writes Raychelle Cassada Lohmann, "the self-infliction of pain reassures them they are still alive. This is especially true when they are experiencing emotional numbness or feeling disconnected from the world around them. Plus, self-harming can cause changes in brain chemistry, which gives the effects of a 'rush' and can easily become addictive and highly dangerous."[2]

While those of us involved in self-harm are not typically suicidal, we risk harming ourselves to the point where we cause medical complications or death, which is precisely why this symptom is so dangerous. And as Mental Health America explains, some people "may become desperate about their lack of control over the behavior and its addictive nature, which may lead them to true suicide attempts."[3]

So What Do We Do?

We shouldn't expect to extinguish an unhealthy coping skill successfully without having a healthy coping skill to replace it with. When we're trying to quit smoking, a behavior we typically engage in to relax or reduce stress, we need to find a behavior that we can engage in every time we *would* pick up a cigarette. This is why people who are trying to quit smoking often chew gum. It's a behavior that replaces cigarettes and isn't unhealthy. Similarly, people engaged in alcohol abuse treatment may drink a lot of soda. Sure, soda may not be all that healthy, but it's definitely a healthier coping skill than self-medicating with alcohol. The whole point is to swap a better behavior for the one we're trying to extinguish.

When it comes to self-harm, we need to learn and practice healthy coping skills that we can engage in during the times we want to self-harm. This isn't easy, mostly because our brain has made a connection between self-harm and feeling some relief.

Some potential replacement behaviors for self-harm follow:

- Put stickers on the parts of your body you want to injure.
- Draw slashing lines on paper.
- Draw on yourself with a red felt-tip pen.
- Take a small bottle of red liquid food coloring and warm it slightly by dropping it in to a cup of hot water for a few minutes. Uncap the bottle and press its tip against the place you want to cut. Draw the bottle in a cutting motion while squeezing it slightly to let the food color trickle out.
- Draw on the areas you want to cut using ice that you've made by dropping six or seven drops of red food coloring into each of the ice-cube-tray wells.
- Paint yourself with red paint.[4]

These behaviors specifically attempt to provide a behavior that is completely safe but gives a similar sensation to that of self-harm.

Coping strategies that don't safely mimic self-harm behavior include taking a bath, reading a book, drinking some tea, playing with a pet, and similar soothing activities that can help us feel calm and better about ourselves and our current situation. The important thing is to find one or more behaviors that we can use in place of self-harm and engage in them whenever the desire to self-harm arises.

Is There Healing and Relief Out There?

Therapy for self-harm primarily focuses on figuring out what underlying issues are present, learning how to better manage our emotions and feelings that lead to us turning to self-harm, and working on growing in our ability to have healthier coping skills to solve our problems and deal with our emotions. In terms of medication, the Mayo Clinic notes that "there are no medications to specifically treat self-injuring behavior. However . . . your doctor may recommend antidepressants or other medications to treat the underlying disorder that's associated with self-injury. Treatment for these disorders may help you feel less compelled to hurt yourself."[5]

What about those of us who are unable to engage in therapy or medication treatment? What kinds of things can we start doing at home to help us push forward to health and wellness?

As with so many other experiences we go through, our journey toward healing starts with figuring out what triggers the desire to self-harm and then developing a plan for soothing ourselves in a healthy manner when those things inevitably come up. As I've mentioned before, this work needs to be done *when we're feeling well*. We cannot expect ourselves to come up with these plans and answers when we're in the throes of our symptoms related to our trauma history, depression, or anxiety.

When we're having a good day, we should sit down with a piece of paper and a pencil, map out things we've noticed as triggering in the past, and then write down what we're going to do when those situations come up. For example, "I usually want to self-harm when my family argues and there's yelling in the house." Then, next to that, we would write something like, "When this happens, I will walk away from the situation and play some music." Having even a simple plan that we can go to when things start to get rough is a big step toward healing and wellness.

What the Bible Says about Self-Harm

> Night and day among the tombs and on the hillsides he was always crying out and bruising himself with stones. Catching sight of Jesus from a distance, he ran up and prostrated himself before him.
>
> —Mark 5:5–6

There is a fine line between self-harm and mortification for the sake of casting off the desires of the flesh and growing in holiness. How do we extol the virtue of a saint from the past who engaged in mortification as a form of penance while seeing self-harm as a dangerous and unhealthy coping mechanism that needs to be treated? How can we tell the difference between the two behaviors? Was St. Rose of Lima, for example, suffering from a desire to self-harm, or was she showing saintly behavior by way of her acceptance of extreme physical penances for Christ?

First, the holy men and women who practiced mortification of the flesh and grew in holiness were doing so under a spiritual director. And whenever a spiritual director advised them to step back from the behavior or calm it down a bit, they listened and were obedient.

Second, the saints who engaged in mortification have gone on to inspire countless Christians. They grew closer to Christ in their lives than most of us could ever imagine, and they dedicated their lives to helping Christ in the poor and suffering and the salvation of souls. Most often, when we're stuck in a cycle of self-harm, we actually feel quite the opposite. We feel isolated, further away from God, and these fruits should alert us to the fact that we are destined for healing and something better.

Cutting is mentioned a few times in the Old Testament, most notably in 1 Kings 18:28 and Deuteronomy 14:1, and was associated with either a practice of mourning or a behavior connected to the worship of idols or false gods. However, we get a glimpse of the idea of mortification in Proverbs 20:30: "Evil is cleansed away by bloody lashes, and a scourging to the inmost being." While these examples exist in scripture, what I'm most interested in highlighting is the example of Christ in Mark 5:1–20. In this story, a man who had been possessed by an unclean spirit comes before Jesus. Jesus casts the spirit out of the man and into a herd of swine, healing him and allowing the man to share the Good News of what Jesus had done for him.

I am not suggesting that our self-harm behavior is connected to possession or unclean spirits. While I'm sure that *can* happen, as it did in the gospel story, I would never assume that self-harm was connected to evil spirits. Instead, I present this story as a way of showing what Jesus offers to those of us who are bound up in unhealthy coping skills, stuck in patterns of behavior that are actually quite harmful for us.

The individual in this story was engaged in self-harm, as the gospel reports: "Night and day among the tombs and on the hillsides he was always crying out and bruising himself with stones" (Mk 5:5). He was engaged in self-harm, Jesus encountered him, and Jesus freed him, healed him, and left him to experience peace and comfort.

We all need to be reminded that Christ desperately wants us to experience peace. He wants to free us from our pain and take away our suffering so that we can experience every good and loving thing he has waiting for us. He wants to come to us through our loved ones, doctors and other helping professionals, and spiritual directors, and he wants to give us freedom, peace, and comfort.

What the Saints Say about Self-Harm

> The gift of grace increases as the struggle increases.
>
> —St. Rose of Lima

Countless saints through the ages have engaged in mortification of the flesh, and we can see the fruits of their spiritual journey still reverberating through our Church. But mortification as a part of the spiritual life and self-harm are not the same thing. St. Catherine of Siena really helps us understand when she writes, "But if the body is weak, fallen into illness, the rule of discretion does not approve of such a method."[6] St. Catherine realized that even holy men and women pursuing mastery over the flesh and the desires of their body could end up in a bad place through the practice of mortification, and she provided an exception to the practice.

St. Gemma Galgani has many instances documented throughout her life where her spiritual director questioned her plans for mortification and advised her to turn back from her plans. Her obedience to his recommendations shows us the importance of spiritual direction if we feel God has called us to this path.

St. Rose of Lima often gets branded as being wrapped up in self-harm because of her taking on of extreme penances. However, I see her more as a tireless advocate and intercessor for us if we are struggling with our journey to healing from self-harm.

Born in 1586 in Peru into a large family, Isabel Flores de Oliva was given the nickname Rose by her parents because of how beautiful she was as a baby. From a young age Rose took on penances, including fasting three times per week. Upset when men admired her beauty, "Rose cut off her hair and smeared pepper on her face."[7] She allowed herself only two hours of sleep per night, devoting the rest of her day to prayer, and "she discovered that she could conceal thorns on the underside of the rose wreath around her head, making the wreath into her own 'crown of thorns.'"[8]

St. Rose of Lima undertook dramatic behaviors in her walk with Christ, but she was also empowered by the Holy Spirit to have the right focus. Through these penances, she grew in her love of the poor, her prayer life, and in other ways that bore fruit down through the generations that would come after her.

Through St. Rose of Lima's prayers, we can receive grace from Christ to reach out for help, move forward on the path of healing, and find the peace God wants us to have.

IN BRIEF

- Per the National Alliance on Mental Illness, "Self-harm is not a mental illness, but a behavior that indicates a need for better coping skills."
- A common misconception is that people engaging in self-harm behaviors are trying to kill themselves. In reality, most of us who

are engaging in self-harm are trying to do something so we can continue living.

- We shouldn't expect to extinguish an unhealthy coping skill successfully without having healthy coping skills to replace it with.
- Therapy for self-harm primarily focuses on figuring out what underlying issues have pushed us into using self-harm as a coping skill, learning how to better manage our emotions and feelings that lead to us turning to self-harm, and working on growing in our ability to have healthier coping skills to solve our problems and deal with our emotions.
- Mortification as a part of the spiritual life and self-harm are not the same thing. The holy men and women who practiced mortification of the flesh and grew in holiness were doing so under a spiritual director. The saints who engaged in mortification have gone on to inspire countless Christians through the generations. They grew closer to Christ in their lives than most of us could ever imagine, and they dedicated their lives to helping Christ in the poor and suffering and the salvation of souls.

CLOSING PRAYER

> Peace I leave with you; my peace I give to you. Not as the world gives do I give it to you. Do not let your hearts be troubled or afraid.
>
> —John 14:27

12. LONELINESS

LORD, THE ONE YOU LOVE IS ISOLATED

When we've been through a traumatic experience, we rightly recognize that it's not something anyone should ever have had to go through. However, we far too often take that correct idea and turn it into, "*Therefore*, no one probably has gone through something like this and there's no one I can connect to or share this with." I've said it, you've probably said it, the Who said it in their 1971 hit "Behind Blue Eyes": no one knows what it's like.

In one sense, no one can know *exactly* what it's like to go through what we've gone through, but there are a whole lot of people who have been through situations like ours, perhaps even identical to ours, who can relate to our thoughts and emotions. If we want someone to know what it's like to go through what we've gone through, we need to connect with those people and talk about it.

When we lost our son in 2016, my desire to isolate from the world was intense. My wife and I had walked through the most difficult situation any parent could face, and I couldn't imagine that anyone would understand what we were going through. To my surprise, pregnancy and infant loss is a widely experienced trauma that *many* parents have walked through. While our stories might be different, the experiences of parents who have lost a pregnancy or an infant are so closely related that we have a bond and connection I find difficult to adequately explain. We share our deepest thoughts, pains, and feelings, no matter how scary they are, and feel comfortable knowing that they will be understood because of that common bond.

Of course, my wife and I would never have found other parents who shared similar losses without sharing our story, speaking openly about our experience, and being vulnerable about our traumatic experience. No one *has* to share what they've gone through. But there comes a time for many of us when we feel more open to sharing our stories. While we've had to weather some weird and uncomfortable responses from time to time, we have come into contact with others who understand our experience on such a deep level. My wife and I never would have found that support if we had pulled the covers over our heads and avoided everyone.

Feeling Isolated Isn't Just Not Wanting to Hang Out

A typical trap of coping with trauma or suffering intense anxiety, depression, or other mental health experiences is isolating ourselves from others. This isolation goes well beyond just not feeling like socializing after a hard day at work or wanting to avoid others after an awkward text-message exchange with friends. It's an intense desire to pull back from our lives, responsibilities, friends, families, and loved ones, and it leads to one of the most dangerous phenomena in our culture today: loneliness.

The term *loneliness* has become such common parlance in today's world that we probably overuse it to describe our experience. Perhaps we say that we feel lonely, when we just need social interaction and support. But true loneliness, true isolation from the world in the face of our mental health experience, is a serious issue. A 2018 study showed that 46 percent of Americans report *always* feeling alone, while 27 percent of Americans say they rarely or never feel as though there are people who actually understand them. In addition, 43 percent of Americans feel that they are isolated from others.[1]

What's the big deal about being lonely? I mean, we all feel lonely from time to time, right? This might sound like a fair question, especially for those of us who haven't been pushed into isolation because of our mental health experience. However, according to the US Department of Veterans Affairs, "loneliness and social isolation may be more robust risk factors for suicide than hopelessness, anxiety, or perceived burdensomeness."[2] This is why the battle against isolation is so serious—we're talking about saving lives.

So What Do We Do?

When suffering a mental health experience, our brain maybe slamming us with the message that our road to recovery will be found in staying away from others and avoiding everything. However, isolation will push us deeper and deeper into our symptoms, even to the point of changing the way our brain is functioning.[3] Instead, we have to fight against what our brain is telling us to do and reach out for support. According to Make the Connection, a resource of the US Department of Veterans Affairs, we can begin to do this in a few ways:

- Address what's causing you to want to be alone.
- Reach out to your friends or family members even though it may be the last thing you feel like doing. Research shows that spending time talking with family or friends improves your mood and has a positive effect on health.
- Connect with . . . groups or participate in clubs or hobbies focused on something you like.[4]

Fighting the intense urge to isolate is so much easier said than done. How do we overcome the desire to pull up the covers and stay away from everyone? Just knowing that we'll feel better by reaching out doesn't automatically lead us to do it, right?

This is one of the pitfalls that many of us find ourselves in when we reach out in therapy. Often, our therapist can help us reach an insight or realization, but our progress stops there. We may better understand what we're experiencing and know that there's an explanation for our experiences, but awareness isn't the entire solution to our problems. We typically have to *act* on that insight. And so it is with realizing that reaching out for social support instead of giving in to isolation will be good for us. But how?

Is There Healing and Relief Out There?

Healing and relief from loneliness comes from reaching out for social support and getting involved with others, once we feel safe, rather than giving into the brain's lie that isolation is good for us. And it starts with small steps to get us engaged.

If you're like me, your knee-jerk reaction to every single invitation that comes by mail, email, or text is to RSVP regrets. But one smart way to push ourselves into socializing with others is to RSVP accepts. This is a passive and easy way to guide ourselves in the right direction in that there's a low bar of what we need to do to make it happen. All we have to do is click yes and show up.

After we've made the decision to start accepting invitations, a great next step is to write down our goals—literally write them down on a piece of paper or in a journal, not just think about them in our head. We might start with a self-assessment of where we're at—how often we're engaging in social interactions or receiving social support—and then come up with some goals for where we'd like to end up. Lower the pressure by setting measurable, accomplishable, and realistic goals, perhaps something as simple as "I will text one person every day to see how they're doing and share how I'm doing," "I will call one friend once each week to check in on them and chat," or "I will go outside at least once per day to feel the sunshine and say hi to the people I see." We can review these goals daily and give ourselves small things to strive for.

"We see indistinctly, as in a mirror" (1 Cor 13:12), St. Paul says. We have a hard time seeing ourselves as we really are. It's hard to analyze our symptoms, figure out how many times we've actually engaged in social interactions (or even wanted to) over the past sixty days, and even remember what we've been eating or how much we've been exercising. Journaling—noting the facts of our days and how we felt about them—can give us baseline data for how we're doing and will help us answer the questions of doctors and therapists if we reach out for their support. It gives us a place to log our goals, recognize when we're doing well and moving toward our goals, and realize when we need additional support, professional or otherwise, when we're having difficulty.

When we reach our goals, we must celebrate our successes and movement toward wellness. I don't care how small it is; celebrate something as simple as clicking yes on an invitation to something social and hoping that you'll feel up to going. It's easy for us to think, *Well, I'm supposed to be doing this, so I don't deserve to be proud of myself.* But every step toward wellness is a step we should be proud of, and every step should be recognized for the strength it took to achieve it.

What the Bible Says about Isolation

> Two are better than one: They get a good wage for their toil. If the one falls, the other will help the fallen one. But woe to the solitary person! If that one should fall, there is no other to help.
>
> —Ecclesiastes 4:9–10

Our brain often makes us believe that isolation is a solution to our problems. As we've established, this is a lie. The Bible reinforces the truth that we need one another, for it tells us that the members of the Body of Christ must lift one another up and not leave anyone behind and that every member has something to give the entire Body.

But isolation is hard to avoid. This seems especially true in today's world, where we seem to know one another less and less and it often seems that those around us don't want to walk with us through our suffering. Sure, St. Paul says, "Bear one another's burdens, and so you will fulfill the law of Christ" (Gal 6:2) and "We urge you, brothers, admonish the idle, cheer the fainthearted, support the weak, be patient with all" (1 Thes 5:14), but when I suffered in the past, I've found that not everyone is open to supporting me.

But then St. Paul says, "For as in one body we have many parts, and all the parts do not have the same function, so we, though many, are one body in Christ and individually parts of one another" (Rom 12:4–5). Here he seems to be sharing that the anecdote for our isolation is not necessarily being open and vulnerable with every person but rather finding the part of the Body of Christ that is meant to be that support for us and opening ourselves up to them. We can fall into the trap of thinking that in order to beat our desire to isolate we have to become overall social individuals. But we can still be selective in whom we open up to and from whom we can expect a supportive relationship. Not every person is going to be able to do that for us, and that's okay; we don't owe our vulnerability to anyone, and everyone doesn't owe their vulnerability to us. Ultimately we only owe it to Christ and, in turn, those who allow Christ to work through them in their lives.

What the Saints Say about Isolation

> If I should become sick and unable to work, then I shall be like the Lord on the cross. He will have mercy on me and help me, I am sure.
>
> —St. Kateri Tekakwitha

Many saints have lived lives marked by isolation and loneliness. So when we feel like there's no one out there who can possibly understand our experience, we can at least turn to some of our holy heroes and ask for their intercession on our behalf before the throne of God.

St. Kateri Tekakwitha had to figure out the path to finding God's love in the midst of loneliness and isolation. She was born in 1676 in the Mohawk village Ossernenon in present-day New York. Her mother was baptized and educated by French missionaries, and she brought her daughter up in the Christian faith. After a smallpox outbreak resulted in the death of her parents and younger brother, Kateri was adopted by her aunt and uncle, who kept her away from anything related to the Christian faith or the missionaries' way of life. They also pushed her to get married.

Kateri refused to get married, though, and this directly resulted in her imposed loneliness, as her family punished her with dangerous threats, harsh ridicule, and an intense workload that was not expected of others.[5] When she was eighteen years old, she met Fr. Jacques de Lamberville. Despite knowing her family's opposition to the Christian faith, she expressed her desire to become a Christian and was baptized just a year later.

When news spread of her official conversion, the ridicule and threats picked up their pace. At one point, she was even accused of sorcery.[6] This atmosphere led to her decision to run away in 1677 to join the Christians at a Jesuit mission just south of Montreal, Quebec.

She prayed and offered up her suffering continuously for the conversion of her family, which is quite incredible considering the suffering, isolation, and loneliness they imposed on her. Her perseverance, incredible trust in Christ, and willingness to continue to pray and stay close to God in the midst of her isolation is a wonderful example to all of us suffering in a similar manner, and St. Kateri is ready and waiting to take our needs to the throne of God for us without hesitation.

IN BRIEF

- When seeking relief from the symptoms of trauma, one of the typical traps we all fall into is isolating ourselves from others.
- If we want to feel better, we've got to fight the intense urge to isolate.
- We can lower the pressure of being around others by making sure to set measurable, accomplishable, and realistic goals, and write down on paper or in a journal the goals we're shooting for.
- "I will text one person every day to see how they're doing and share how I'm doing," "I will call one friend once each week to check in on them and just have a chat," or "I will go outside at least once per day just to feel the sunshine and say hi to people I see" are small goals to write down, review daily, and give yourself small things to strive for.

CLOSING PRAYER

> Behold, the virgin shall be with child and bear a son, and they shall name him Emmanuel, which means "God is with us."
>
> —Matthew 1:23

RELATIONSHIPS

13. RESENTMENT

LORD, THE ONE YOU LOVE IS KEEPING SCORE

Our first child was a colicky baby, and my wife and I weren't prepared for how the emotional ups and downs, the anxiety of not knowing what to do, and the dread of being alone with a baby put stress on our relationship. One of the ways that stress manifested in our life was in the idea of keeping score. Our son cried *a lot* in the middle of the night, and when we would shift-change during those times, we would easily fall victim to being resentful of the other—resentful if they didn't try to soothe him for what we thought was a long enough time, resentful if they didn't try to soothe him in a manner that we thought was best, and (believe it or not) resentful if they were able to get him back to sleep after we had been unsuccessful moments earlier.

People warn new parents about how they'll always be tired, but being tired had nothing on the pressure all of this resentment put on our relationship.

What is it about our desire to have fairness in a relationship or to spend time keeping score in order to show that things aren't fair? Why do we do this to ourselves? Why have we imbibed the idea that an ideal relationship is meant to be fifty-fifty rather than each partner at 100 percent as our Church teaches?

It's important to recognize that, at a basic level, this is just a part of our human nature. We have a seemingly ingrained sense of fairness and a desire to see that fairness play out in specific ways. We can see this in young children fighting with their siblings over who got the most fruit snacks. It's a part of life that we have to experience and learn to work through. But when it comes to relationships, keeping score and becoming resentful over a perceived lack of fairness can be poisonous.

Being Resentful Is Not the Same as Getting Frustrated

All of us will experience times of frustration in our relationships. (This is true for all kinds of relationships, but I'm going to focus on romantic partnerships in this part of the book.) After all, we're constantly learning how to give and accept love, and learning how to love another person as God loves them gives us daily opportunities to see where we're lacking and where we need to improve.

When a partner leaves the toilet seat up or doesn't take out the trash in time for the morning collection, we might get frustrated. Similarly, when we leave our clothes on the floor or accidentally throw away important paperwork or track mud in the house, our partner might get frustrated with us. That frustration can lead to arguments, and it's a bad feeling for everyone involved. Again, we're all trying our best to move forward and grow as individuals in relationships with the hopes of learning to let go of the small frustrations and focus on loving others unconditionally. But it ain't easy.

Resentment, however, is on a whole different level. This idea of keeping score, a game we have all played in our relationships from time to time, can poison a relationship. When we're always on the lookout for fairness and equality in the tasks around the house, for example, we can always find ways to feel we're being cheated and then start to grow in resentment toward our partner.

Harboring resentment against someone is dangerous because it leads directly to a disconnect in our ability to have empathy for them. After all, if I see the relationship as my partner failing to shoulder what I deem is an equal responsibility in the family, why would I ever try to put myself in their shoes and try to feel what it's like to be on their side of things? Once our ability to have empathy for our partner fades away, the warning lights start going off and something needs to be done quickly to refocus the relationship and get things back on track.

So What Do We Do?

Communication is key to healing from resentment in a relationship. It's not hard, but it is something we have to actively work on, especially because the things that bother us might not bother the other person, or we might not hear what the other person is actually trying to communicate.

The things that bother us and what we think have to get done may not be the same things that bother our partner or that they feel have to get done. Our typical approach to solving this problem is to nag our partner in an effort to get them to comply with what we want them to do, which builds resentment at both ends. We feel we shouldn't have to nag our partner just to get them to do something as obvious as picking up their clothes off the floor. They get frustrated at being nagged for something as unimportant as leaving some clothes laying around.

To fend off resentment, we have to communicate what things are important to us and why. We can't expect our partner to read our mind. We have to tell them what things we value, what things we have grown to expect in relationships because of our past experiences, *and we have to tell them why*. It isn't enough to say, "I can't stand you leaving your clothes on the floor!" because if clothes on the floor doesn't bother our partner, they'll just think we're weird for having a problem with it. We have to share the reason this bothers us as well.

This insight into our thinking will help foster a healthier dialogue. Our partner may respond, "I see where you're coming from and I'll try to be more conscious of this," or they will share their viewpoint for why they don't see it as an issue, and we can then seek some kind of compromise or at least understanding.

Another approach to avoiding or healing resentment is to *do it yourself*. I'm not suggesting you should do *everything* yourself but rather that you think about the small things that happen in your life that breed resentment (such as the clothes on the floor). Wouldn't doing the things we want to have done rather than nagging and harboring resentments go a long way toward maintaining a peaceful relationship? Let's face it, picking up a shirt and tossing it in the hamper ends the whole problem right there. You've just kept a five-second task from spilling into an argument that could last well into the night and potentially foster a lot of resentment.

Sometimes resentment builds in a relationship because we don't hear what our partner is saying or we misunderstand what they mean to convey. Active listening is a skill often suggested in couples therapy to address this, and it really works. When in a conversation with active listening as a goal, we sit *next* to, rather than across from, our partner. Sitting next to our partner is a nonverbal way of showing that we're in this together. Next, we hold hands, which can be hard when we're engaged in a difficult conversation, but holding hands goes a long way toward cutting the tension and making us think twice before saying something hurtful.

The most important skills of active listening are listening, paraphrasing what we have heard, and being willing to listen when our partner corrects what we've heard. It takes effort to learn to listen to our partner instead of focusing on our thoughts or formulating our response, but it makes all the difference. We quietly listen to what they're saying *and then* before responding with our own thoughts, we paraphrase what we've heard them say: "So what I hear you saying is . . ." Once we relay what we think we've heard back to them, we give our partner space to correct it with what they actually meant, just in case we misunderstood them.

Our interpretation of what our partner has said so often misses the mark on what they were actually trying to say. For example, our partner might say, "It really bothers me that you leave your clothes laying around on the floor." We hear, "You are disgusting and dirty and not worthy of love." Okay, that might sound like a bit much, but it's not too far from the truth. We hear something critical about one small part of our life, one small thing we've done or didn't do, and we extrapolate it to mean that our partner finds us to be an absolute failure.

Thankfully, this active listening technique can help us get closer to hearing what they actually mean:

> "It really bothers me that you leave your clothes laying around on the floor."

> "So what I hear you saying is that I'm dirty and leave our house messy and you're disappointed in me."
>
> "No, actually, I think you do a great job keeping the house picked up; it's just this one little thing."

Once we hear what our partner is actually trying to say, it's typically just limited to a small issue that can be corrected rather easily, and it's rarely as catastrophic as the thing we've made up in our head. But does this method always work?

Is There Healing and Relief Out There?

Active listening always works if . . .

Of course, there's always an "if," and in this circumstance, it always works *if* we're willing to believe that what our partner is saying is true. That's the hard part. We have become so sure of our assessment of conversations, what people are trying to say to us, what people think of us, that even when they straight-up tell us what they mean, *we don't believe them*!

Our mind tilts toward the negative, and that's where resentment forms. If we want healing and relief from our resentments in our relationships, we have to assume good intentions. We have to ditch the desire to interpret what we read between the lines and believe them.

Sharing how we're feeling, not expecting our partner to read our mind, taking responsibility for tasks that are priorities for us (just do it!), sitting next to each other and holding hands, and believing that we are worthy of love and that our partner believes that too—these are the keys toward finding healing and relief from the resentments that plague our mind and tear apart our relationships.

Couples therapy is a fantastic aid in learning how to use these coping skills, especially active listening. Being able to practice active listening with a therapist allows us to learn the skills in a safe environment, and the therapist can provide a valuable outside perspective on the relationship and the way it has been functioning. According to the psychologist Dianne Grande, couples therapy has been found to be "roughly 75 percent effective," which is true across cultures and for "high-stress clients such as military couples, veterans with PTSD, parents of chronically ill children, and infertile couples."[1]

What the Bible Says about Resentment

> All bitterness, fury, anger, shouting, and reviling must be removed from you, along with all malice. [And] be kind to one another, compassionate, forgiving one another as God has forgiven you in Christ.
>
> —Ephesians 4:31–32

Throughout scripture, we are reminded that harboring resentments, focusing on things that make us upset, and refusing to forgive or give someone the benefit of the doubt is a recipe for disaster in our walk with Christ. There is no room for repaying small inconveniences with resentment, anger, or even thoughts of frustration toward our partner.

Of course, it's much easier said than done. How do we fight against our selfish and fallen human nature? How do we make the decision to live at peace with everyone and overlook an offense when our minds are telling us to get upset, stand up for fairness and equality in our relationships, and be resentful?

I'm reminded of the words of Christ in Matthew 19:26: "For human beings this is impossible, but for God all things are possible"; and then again his words from Matthew 11:28–30: "Come to me, all you who labor and are burdened, and I will give you rest. Take my yoke upon you and learn from me, for I am meek and humble of heart; and you will find rest for yourselves. For my yoke is easy, and my burden light."

There is real power and freedom to be found in placing everything on Christ, giving him every resentment we hold in our hearts and saying, "Here you go, help!" He can help, he can give us the strength to live in peace with everyone, and he wants us to cast our burdens on him. This isn't just the classic "Offer it up" we heard so often growing up in the Catholic Church, but rather "Trust him to help you." He will not abandon us to our anger, he will not turn a blind eye to our suffering, and he will not ignore our true desire to be free from resentment. He wants to show us the way, if only we ask and commit to following his lead. It is only through him that we can truly release the power resentment has over our relationships.

What the Saints Say about Resentment

> Let me, my Jesus, share in your suffering, at least one of your thorns.
>
> —St. Rita of Cascia

St. Augustine really drives home the destructive power of resentment: "Resentment is like taking poison and hoping the other person dies." The resentments we hold, either in the silence of our hearts or that we say out loud in moments of frustration, have the potential to rot our relationships from the inside out. When we recognize what we're doing to ourselves and our partner, we have to be willing to fight back against our inclinations toward resentment, root it out, and join our partner in moving the relationship to a healthier and more peaceful place.

It can give us pause when we look to the lives of various saints who clung to our Lord, avoided resentments even in the direst circumstances, and overcame every sinful inclination to push through life in inspiring ways.

One such holy hero is St. Rita of Cascia. Rita was born in 1381 in Italy. Her parents were noble and yet known to be charitable. Despite her early requests to be admitted to a local convent, her parents arranged a marriage for her at the age of twelve. While arranged marriages at this age were somewhat common at the time, her experience was not a happy one. Her husband was physically and verbally abusive, and he had affairs for many years.

No one would have judged her for harboring resentments given all the abuse and difficulty she had to face at the hands of her husband, and yet she persevered in her holiness and humility in spite of it all. When her husband was murdered eighteen years into their marriage, Rita forgave his murderers and prayed that their twin sons, who wanted to avenge their father's death, would also forgive them, which they did before their own early deaths. Free from her husband, Rita was finally able to join the convent, and she spent the last forty years of her life in the Augustinian convent at Cascia. Fifteen years before her death, "she received a stigmata-like thorn wound in answer to her prayers to be more profoundly conformed to the passion of the Lord Jesus. Rita was bedridden for the last four years of her life, consuming almost nothing except for the Eucharist. She died of tuberculosis at the age of seventy on May 22, 1456."[2]

St. Rita is an incredible example of someone who turned her difficulties into opportunities, always thinking of ways to turn toward Christ for help rather than falling into a cycle of resentment even in these most difficult of circumstances. She's also an example of someone who, when her circumstances changed, used the opportunity to chase her dream rather than remain mired in resentment over not being able to live out that dream sooner. She used her strength through Christ to overcome any selfishness or resentments.

St. Rita is ready to intercede for all of us who find ourselves tempted to resentment in our own relationships. It's worth it to reach out to her, someone who knows what it's like to experience precisely these kinds of struggles, and ask her to implore Jesus to give us his grace, his peace, and his life.

IN BRIEF

- Keeping score, a game we have all played in our relationships from time to time, is one of the most concerning things to come up in a relationship.
- Resentment and harboring thoughts of resentment toward our partner leads directly to a disconnect in our ability to have empathy for them.
- We have to communicate what is important to us and why. The time for holding resentment toward our partner because they don't do something we want them to do, even though we've never told them it bothers us, has to end.
- Active listening involves listening, paraphrasing what we have heard, and being willing to listen when our partner corrects what we've heard. It takes effort to learn to listen to our partner instead of focusing on our thoughts or formulating a response in haste, but it makes all the difference.

- Couples therapy is a fantastic aid in learning how to use these coping skills, especially active listening.

CLOSING PRAYER

> When you stand to pray, forgive anyone against whom you have a grievance, so that your heavenly Father may in turn forgive you your transgressions.
>
> —Mark 11:25

14. FEELING STAGNANT

LORD, THE ONE YOU LOVE IS GOING NOWHERE . . . FAST

We've all been there: the kids are asleep, we have our first opportunity to be alone with our partner in what feels like weeks, an opportunity to be romantic, be loving, or just simply talk like we used to. But instead of doing any of that, we flip on the TV and zone out without a word for the next two hours and then collapse into bed. And it plays out again and again every night.

When we don't take the time to work on our relationship, to make an effort to share and accept love, we quickly realize that we're going nowhere *fast*. That feeling of things being stagnant can become a suffocating experience that feels like it might be the initial step toward walking away from the whole thing.

That relationships take effort may be a cliché, but we know in our hearts it's true. We can't ignore our relationships and expect them to thrive. We can't put things on autopilot and expect love to flourish.

The problem is that sometimes we're just so burned out from the daily responsibilities of life that we don't feel we have the ability to put the effort in. And it is okay that we feel that way sometimes. We just need to recognize what's going on and then be willing to look at ways to cope with the feeling so we can get things back on track.

The saying that you can't take care of someone until you take care of yourself applies in this situation. If you're burned out, depressed, or struggling with life in general, it's going to be hard to put the effort into your relationship to push it from stagnant to thriving. So, if you're finding this to be the case, flip back to the earlier chapter that seems to line up best with what you're going through, work through that issue as best as you can, and then start to put the effort into your relationship. Of course, you've got to be open and honest with your partner as you do this.

A Relationship Becoming Stagnant Is More than Just Being Bored with Each Other

There's a difference between things being stagnant in a relationship and simply being bored with each other at any given time. Being bored in a relationship can pop up for various reasons, and it happens to all of us from time to time. We all get into ruts: going to the same place for date night and having the same conversations. Relationships go through cycles; sometimes we might feel bored, and that's okay.

Our relationship becoming stagnant, on the other hand, is more like a cancer that sneaks in, grows because of our permission, and festers in all of our interactions because of our acceptance. If we allow that stagnation to continue, it will push us further and further into irritation, arguments, and cold behavior, from which it can be difficult to come back.

A relationship that is becoming stagnant doesn't necessarily have blow-out fights, angry words, or a partner sleeping on the couch. Instead, it involves a lot of autopilot behavior—the routines we carry out without giving much thought to them.

An *avoidance* of conflict can also tip us off to our relationship becoming stagnant. When our relationship becomes stagnant, we can typically be nice to each other most of the time, and we might even compromise quickly to avoid negative feelings. While it seems counterintuitive, a willingness to enter into conversations that can get heated or emotional can actually be a good sign in a relationship. When we've decided to give in to the stagnant experience, we typically don't care to engage in such conversations, so take heart that your arguments might actually be a good sign!

All that being said, living a life on autopilot, allowing our relationships to become stagnant, eventually starts to grind away on us. And eventually we realize that we have to do something.

So What Do We Do?

To address a stagnant relationship, we have to start slow. We have to ask each other what would be helpful and set attainable goals. Of course we want things to go from zero to one hundred really quickly, but that's not how life works. Especially if we've been stuck in this stagnant phase for weeks, months, or even years, it's going to take time and dedication to get the relationship going again. We have to be reasonable with our expectations and take one step at a time.

Asking our partner what they think would be helpful is one of the most overlooked healthy coping skills when we find ourselves in this situation. We may spend time trying to cook up plans to help alleviate the stagnancy without really understanding what the problem is. Or perhaps our partner has a specific way that they receive love that would help them feel the relationship is moving in the right direction, but we show them love in a different way and we miss the connection altogether. We aren't going to get very far in our efforts unless we make sure we're starting on the same page.

Along with communication, some simple ideas to work on at home that can help heal the stagnancy include staying positive, discussing things we're grateful for, making a conscious effort to stop assuming we know what our partner is thinking, and actively trying to help each other. If we focus on and talk about our blessings in life, and in this case our relationship, we will maintain a more positive attitude. Even in the midst of a stagnant relationship, we can be grateful for our safety, a partner who has been with us, comfort of companionship, being able to be ourselves in front of another, and someone to have meals with. Even the smallest of blessings can shift our focus away from the stagnant feeling we've been experiencing and help us to stay positive and hopeful.

We can't read our partner's mind, *no matter how long we've been with them*. I know we all think that we know what our partner is thinking and feeling all the time, but we don't! This idea that we can see through their words to what they're really thinking is dangerous because it leads us to work off of assumptions that aren't true. We have to talk! We have to actively listen and reflect back what we think we're hearing, allow our partner to clear up the assumptions we have developed, and believe what our partner says. It takes practice, and it takes slowing down, but the benefits can turn things around faster than you might believe.

Lastly, we have to actively help each other out. Going out of our way to be thoughtful is a big key toward showing love, commitment, and care for our partner. Filling up a tank of gas without being asked, helping to make sure they have a glass of water by their bedside before they hit the sack, and folding their laundry and actually putting it away for them are all examples of tiny little surprises that cost us almost nothing to do (other than five minutes of selfless behavior) and have huge payoff in our relationship because they help our partner feel understood, appreciated, and loved. And imagine how powerful small acts like these can be in the midst of a stagnant relationship, where tensions and irritability run high!

Is There Healing and Relief Out There?

When we're going through it, it can feel like getting a stagnant relationship back to the way it used to be is impossible. We might find that we're unable to pull ourselves out of this situation on our own. In these instances, we have to find the strength to reach out for help. Couples therapy can feel like letting a stranger into your most intimate and personal relationship and admitting that you can't figure out how to make it work in a way that's healthy for everyone involved. That's scary! But a therapist is an objective observer from outside the relationship, without any emotional attachment other than empathy and wanting you both to thrive. And I can assure you that there's nothing you can bring to therapy as a couple that a therapist hasn't heard before and helped other couples through.

For Catholics specifically, there's a lot of fear that going to couples therapy may result in the therapist recommending the couple split, and sadly that keeps a lot of us from reaching out for help. It's worth remembering that a therapist's goal is to help you live the life you want to live; likewise, a couples therapist is going to engage in treatment with the goal of helping your relationship get wherever you want it to go. If you're a Catholic couple who prioritizes working through even the most difficult circumstances and staying together for life, *tell your therapist that* right at the outset of therapy.

A couples therapist will most likely help you pinpoint the root cause of the issue being presented to therapy. They'll coach you in some basic communication work, similar to the reflective and active listening covered in the previous chapter. Finally, they'll help you develop healthier interactions, become more deeply connected on an emotional level, and strengthen the bond that has become stagnant.

It's powerful. It's worth it. And above all, it really helps.

What the Bible Says about Feeling Stagnant

> The one who sat on the throne said, "Behold, I make all things new."
>
> —Revelation 21:5

God understands human nature. He understands that we will find ourselves in stagnant relationships, either with our partner or even with God himself. He knows this and yet he still loves us, he still wants us to push forward through the difficulty, and he gives us the means to do it, through his grace and those around us who are able to help us move forward.

There's a thread through both the Old and the New Testaments of something new happening through God. Do we perceive when God moves to do something new, to offer something new and beautiful into our lives? When people have an inkling of being interested in therapy but decide against it because of the stigma associated with therapy or for some other more practical reason, I think about this message from God in Isaiah: "Now it springs forth, do you not perceive it?" (Is 43:19).

God moves us in subtle and quiet ways, and it can be hard for us to correctly identify what he's trying to do in our lives. He deeply wants us to be well, for our relationships to thrive and to be focused on holiness and heaven. He wants us to freely leave behind the past that has been holding us back and embrace what goodness he has waiting for us.

Let's find the strength to open that door, see what God is making new in us, and walk through.

What the Saints Say about Feeling Stagnant

> O Jesus, how are You doing in the narrow cell of my heart? Are You alright? Expand my chest, because it is no longer enough to contain You. . . . Jesus, allow me to pour out my affections with You.
>
> —St. Gemma Galgani

While we may be willing to admit and share the experience of our relationships becoming stagnant, we may be more reluctant to say the same about our relationship with God. If we're always trying to grow in holiness, we wouldn't dare allow our relationship with Christ to grow stagnant, right? It's sad that we keep this one locked up and refuse to share it. If we opened up about how our relationship with God can grow stagnant at times, we'd find a great community of others who have experienced this, who can help and guide us in how to push forward to a thriving relationship with God, just as we're trying to do with our partner.

The saints can be an integral part of that community. In their lives and stories we can read about their experiences of stagnancy with God and others, and then see what they learned through those experiences about keeping those relationships healthy and flourishing. As St. Elizabeth Ann Seton said, "God is like a looking glass in which souls see each other. The more united we are to him by love, the nearer we are to those who belong to him."

Of course we see the importance of prayer, spiritual reading, and staying close to the sacraments. In addition to these practices, we see the lives of the saints as shining examples that we can imitate in ways that make sense in our own lives. We can call on our friends in heaven for help in our time of need, sure that they will intercede for God's will to be done in our relationships and our lives in general.

One such saint is St. Gemma Galgani. Born in 1878 in Italy, Gemma was the fifth of eight children. Her family made the decision, soon after her birth, to uproot and move to the city of Lucca to help give the children a chance at a better education. Unfortunately, it was also at this time that her family went through a difficult trial, as first Gemma's mother was diagnosed with tuberculosis, which later killed her, and several of Gemma's siblings died. Then, when Gemma was just sixteen years old, she contracted spinal meningitis, but was miraculously cured thanks to the intercession of St. Gabriel of Our Lady of Sorrows and St. Margaret Mary Alacoque. Just two years later, her father died and she was left an orphan.

Her experience of suffering after suffering led her into a deep and mystical relationship with our Lord, and in fact, she began to experience the stigmata at the age of twenty-one. She also experienced visitations from our Lord, our Lady, and her guardian angel in which she conversed with all of them. She also experienced at least one instance of levitating so she could hug the crucifix hung on the wall with both of her arms in a deep embrace.

Gemma became so close to Christ that she once remarked, "I am happy in every way that Jesus wills, and if Jesus wants the sacrifice of my life, I give it to Him at once. If he wants anything else, I am ready. One thing alone is enough for me; to be his victim, in order to atone for my innumerable sins, and if possible, for those of the whole world."[1] Her perseverance in the face of incredible trials, her refusal to allow her relationship with Christ to become stagnant or broken even in the face of things that would make the best of us crumble, and her positive outlook on everything because of him whom she willingly suffered for makes her an incredible patron to those of us wanting to leave behind those feelings of stagnancy and move forward into loving, selfless, thriving relationships. Her intercession is vital for those of us trying to help our partners get to heaven. She understood what it took to have a deep and intense relationship with Christ, and we can follow her in our own small way toward him and toward a more healthy and happy relationship.

IN BRIEF

- We can't ignore our relationships and expect them to thrive. We can't put things on autopilot and expect love to flourish.
- Stagnancy in a relationship is like a cancer that grows because of our permission and festers in all of our interactions because of our acceptance.
- In order to fix stagnation in a relationship, we must start slow and ask each other what would be helpful.
- We have to actively help each other out. Going out of our way to be thoughtful is a way to show our love, commitment, and care for our partner.
- If you've been waiting for a push to get you and your partner to reach out for help, especially in the form of couples therapy, consider this that push.

CLOSING PRAYER

> People are made for happiness. Rightly, then, you thirst for happiness. Christ has the answer to this desire of yours. But He asks you to trust Him.
>
> —Pope John Paul II

15. MANIPULATIVE RELATIONSHIPS

LORD, THE ONE YOU LOVE IS BEING EXPLOITED

One of the most difficult issues to tackle as a therapist is to help someone recognize and then navigate through a manipulative relationship—namely, helping a person understand that they don't deserve to be in a relationship like this, that they aren't to blame for their circumstance, and that there are steps they can take to work through the current situation to find health and well-being.

Why is it that a manipulative partner leads us to question ourselves so deeply? How can they get us to believe that we don't have the right to be treated with respect, to express our own thoughts and desires, to politely say no without feeling bad afterward, and to be safe, healthy, and happy? How can they make us doubt our own perceptions? This is how deeply destructive a manipulative partner can be. Not only do they use us to get they want, not only do they exploit our insecurities and weaknesses, but also they do it all while making it feel like it's our fault. And while being with a manipulative partner isn't a mental health experience like depression or anxiety is, the long-term effects that come from such a relationship—one in which we don't feel safe, supported, or as if we matter—can definitely harm our mental health.

As Catholics, we can have a difficult time recognizing we're being manipulated and making the difficult decision to do something about it. We aim to fulfill Christ's call to love unconditionally, to think of others before ourselves, and to pour ourselves out for our loved ones without considering the cost. But Jesus doesn't want us to be manipulated or used as a tool for another getting what they want when they want it. Being a good Christian doesn't mean we're called to be a doormat.

While Christ calls us to give 100 percent to our sisters and brothers, he also calls our sisters and brothers to give 100 percent to us. We are to help each other grow in holiness and embrace the gift of salvation Christ offers us. This is especially true in our most intimate relationships. We aren't meant to give everything we have to another at the expense of our emotional, mental, or physical well-being.

Being Manipulative Isn't Just Having Influence

It can be difficult to recognize when we're being manipulated by a partner, so it's important to define what a manipulative relationship is, what manipulative behavior looks like, and how to identify a partner who may be manipulating us.

The communication coach Preston Ni defines psychological manipulation as "the exercise of undue influence through mental distortion and emotional exploitation, with the intention to seize power, control, benefits, and privileges at the victim's expense."[1] One way to recognize a manipulative relationship is to look internally at how we're left feeling after an interaction with our partner. When we're in a manipulative relationship, we experience feelings such as fear, obligation, and guilt that can help tip us off to what's going on.[2] We fear letting the other person down, that they might leave us if we don't do what they ask, and that we are a bad person. We're overcome with a sense of obligation, feeling as though we have to do what they say because we're in a relationship with them. And we feel guilty if we consider saying no to a request. We desire to chase off the guilt by any means necessary, most often by always saying yes just to keep that guilty feelings at bay.

When we recognize that we're in a manipulative relationship, it's easy to blame ourselves. How could we not have seen this? How did we let this happen? And then we usually go to the next level of thought, which is "I deserve this." In reality, no one is to blame for finding themselves in a manipulative relationship. In fact, it can happen to any of us because manipulators are masters at getting what they want at our expense. They know how to detect weaknesses, use them against us, convince us to give up parts of ourselves for them, and continue to get what they want until we put a stop to it.[3]

Ways that these manipulative partners do their dirty work include

- withholding sex or affection;
- withholding money or something of value;
- making you feel shame, embarrassment, or guilt;
- crying;
- withdrawing or avoiding;
- giving the silent treatment;
- pouting;
- whining;
- having a temper tantrum;
- doling out threats and ultimatums;
- lying or twisting the truth;
- criticizing and disapproving;
- being vague about wants or needs;
- blaming;
- being coercive;
- showing exaggerated disappointment;
- withholding or hiding information; and
- twisting your words (or their meaning).[4]

A healthy, thriving, and mutually respectful relationship where the partners are intent on helping each other grow in holiness and make it to heaven won't have these coercive patterns of behavior. Most of us whine or pout from time to time, but when there are numerous episodes of these behaviors present and they are used by the other person to get what they want, then we know there is a problem in the relationship. In fact, sometimes just being presented with a list of manipulative behaviors helps us realize that we've been involved in just such a relationship in the past, or perhaps even presently. It can be difficult to accept, and it can leave us wondering what we can do to help get our relationship back on track.

So What Do We Do?

Manipulation in a relationship like we're discussing here is a form of emotional abuse and is never okay. It's an unhealthy way to interact in a relationship, most likely learned through experiences from earlier in life, even possibly by watching the way one's parents interacted.

So what can we do if we find ourselves in a relationship like this and we want to start moving things in the right direction? We must first recognize a maladaptive behavior for what it is.

I think it's only fair that we give even manipulative partners the benefit of the doubt by considering that they may be operating on autopilot because of the way they've developed their sense of being in a relationship. This isn't to condone or justify the behavior but rather to help us see that people who are manipulating us may not truly understand what they're doing and how they're harming us. This, of course, does not apply to manipulative behavior that is intentional; instead, it focuses on learned behaviors that lead one to be manipulative without realizing what they're doing. The first step to helping them understand is to provide some insight.

To get the point across in the most effective way possible, we've got to be sure to use our best communication techniques to let our partner know what's happening and that it isn't going to continue. Using "I" statements—focusing on how we feel and how their behavior affects us rather than on what they are doing wrong—is one effective way to do that. With "I" statements we help the listener be open to the message rather than immediately feeling defensive and closing off to the message. This communication approach can be difficult, mostly because the emotions we're going through make us just want to stand up and scream, "You're ruining my life!" While screaming can be absolutely justified in a situation like this, it's not going to help our partner receive the message. So we need to take a deep breath, get our "I" statements ready, and let our partner know how we feel.

Calling out the behavior, once established within the relationship, needs to happen in the moment: "Hang on, I'm feeling like this is a little manipulative or coercive." That often stops the behavior in its tracks, and if our partner has good intentions, can lead to corrective behavior.

In addition to recognizing manipulative behavior and calling it out using effective communication, we must treat this behavior as a big deal that must be worked through and dealt with. If we call out the manipulation but shrug it off as small potatoes after a little push back, we send the message that it's not something serious. Instead, we have to be sure to point out it's happening and clearly state that it isn't acceptable. We can't let a manipulative partner tell us we're blowing it out of proportion or that we're grumpy because we had a bad day. Our partner has to hear that this behavior needs to be resolved if the relationship is going to be healthy and continue.

Is There Healing and Relief Out There?

When we find ourselves in a manipulative relationship, and it's a relationship that we want to find a healthy way of continuing, couples therapy has got to jump to the top of our to-do list. Couples therapy provides not only an outside observer who can give emotionally neutral thoughts on the relationship but also a safe space for tough conversations to take place.

A therapist will help prompt active listening reflections and questions for clarification and guide the conversation to ensure it's effective. They will also help us learn these skills so that we can use them at home. After all, skills that we learn in therapy are only as effective as how well we use them on the other six days of the week!

Preston Ni explains a way we might learn to communicate as we work to get our relationship back where it needs to be:

> When you hear an unreasonable solicitation, it's sometimes useful to put the focus back on the manipulator by asking a few probing questions, to see if she or he has enough self-awareness to recognize the inequity of their scheme. For example:
>
> - Does this seem reasonable to you?
> - Does what you want from me sound fair?
> - Do I have a say in this?
> - Are you asking me or telling me?
> - So, what do I get out of this?

- Are you really expecting me to [restate the inequitable request]?[5]

Once we recognize the behavior and express the need for change, these questions are a healthy way for us to engage in conversation that continues to expose and root out manipulative behavior.

Remember, reaching out for couples therapy is a sign of strength, not weakness. It shows that we care enough about our partner and our relationship to learn new skills to help get back on a healthy path. As long as we're safe (emotionally, physically, sexually, mentally, financially, and culturally), it's always worth it to pursue therapy to see how we can grow in health and wellness with our partner.

In a situation where our partner may be consciously taking steps to manipulate us, we must prioritize our safety and the safety of our children (if we have any). If our safety is in question, we must reach out to our support system to get the help we need to ensure our safety. Once we're in a situation where we have that sense of safety again, we can then look toward exploring couples therapy as a viable path or determine that maintaining some distance for the sake of everyone's safety is the appropriate approach.

What the Bible Says about Manipulation

> . . . not to take advantage of or exploit a brother in this matter, for the Lord is an avenger in all these things, as we told you before and solemnly affirmed. For God did not call us to impurity but to holiness.
>
> —1 Thessalonians 4:6–7

God values freedom. He values freedom in his relationship with us and in our relationships with others. God does not want us to be manipulated by our partners, treated unfairly, or deceived. In addition, God wants us to *do something* when we're being manipulated. And when we're caught in a manipulative relationship, God is desperately trying to reach us through loved ones, helping professionals, and fellow Catholics who care about us.

While scripture is clear about the sin of manipulation, it's also clear about hope. Sometimes we can feel hopeless when we first recognize we're in a manipulative relationship, and maybe have been for some years. Those feelings of guilt and shame can be overwhelming. But our God is a God of hope, and the Christian faith is one healing and redemption.

God realizes how hard it is to take action, to stand up for ourselves, to have a fruitful conversation that gets to the point and leads us to happiness. He knows the human heart. He knows all of our emotions, our guilt, and our reservations.

What the Saints Say about Manipulation

> Hold your eyes on God and leave the doing to him. That is all the doing you have to worry about.
>
> —St. Jane Frances de Chantal

It can be difficult to distinguish between unconditional love and codependency and allowing ourselves to be manipulated. Sometimes we might miss the fact that we're involved in a manipulative relationship because we see it as pouring ourselves out for our partner, giving everything we have to help them and love them, and we conclude that this is what Christ wants us to do.

On the day before Bl. Charles of Austria's wedding to his wife, Zita, he said to her, "Now let's help each other get into heaven." Everything that happens in our relationship with our partner must be viewed through this lens. This is the purpose of our relationships, both marriage and friendships: to help each other get to heaven. If things are happening in our relationship—manipulative behavior, for example—that are antithetical to that goal and purpose, we can be sure that they should be cast aside.

St. Jane Frances de Chantal is a holy hero who can give us strength when evaluating our relationships, as she lived through some seriously difficult manipulative relationships even in the midst of grief.

St. Jane Frances de Chantal was born in 1572 in France. Her mother died when she was just eighteen months old. She was married at the age of twenty-one to a baron, Christopher de Rabutin Chantal, moved into his castle, and had six children, three of whom died in infancy. While living at the castle, she brought the faith back to the area: daily

Mass started happening again, and she engaged in charitable works to show the love God had for all his children.

Her husband was killed after seven years of marriage, and Jane became depressed and filled with grief. Her father-in-law then manipulated her to return to his home by threatening disinheriting her children. After putting up with this manipulative relationship that caused her anguish, grief, and spiritual desolation, Jane met St. Francis de Sales and her life was forever changed. She found her heart set ablaze by his words. After working with him through spiritual direction, which included making the decision to continue to care for her father-in-law, she went on to found the Congregation of the Visitation, a religious order that had eighty-six houses at the time of her death in 1641.

St. Jane Frances de Chantal shows us that it is possible to have been in a manipulative relationship and yet not let that relationship define us. I see it as a sign of great hope that God can still work marvels and wonders in our lives in spite of all of our trials. And it brings me even more hope that we all have friends in heaven who understand our experience and know exactly what to beg God for on our behalf, no questions or explanations necessary.

IN BRIEF

- As Catholics, we can have a difficult time recognizing we're being manipulated and making the difficult decision to do something about it. We aim to fulfill Christ's call to love unconditionally, to think of others before ourselves, and to pour ourselves out for our loved ones without considering the cost. But Jesus doesn't want us to be manipulated.
- When we recognize that we're in a manipulative relationship, it's easy to blame ourselves. In reality, no one is to blame for finding themselves in a manipulative relationship.
- Manipulation in a relationship like we're discussing here is a form of emotional abuse and is never okay.

- Manipulative behavior needs to be eliminated from our relationships, and the first step to eliminating a maladaptive behavior is to recognize it and call it what it is.
- Remember, reaching out for couples therapy is a sign of strength, not weakness. It shows that we care enough about our partner and our relationship to learn new skills to help get back on a healthy path. As long as we're safe—emotionally, physically, sexually, mentally, financially, and culturally—it's always worth it to pursue therapy to see how we can grow in health and wellness with our partner.

CLOSING PRAYER

> A person's rightful due is to be treated as an object of love, not as an object for use.
>
> —Pope John Paul II

16. ABUSIVE RELATIONSHIPS

LORD, THE ONE YOU LOVE IS BEING HARMED

A well-known stereotype of Catholics is that we never get divorced. Of all the possible stereotypes about us that could permeate our culture, we have to agree that this is a pretty positive one. After all, in Matthew 5:31–32 Jesus clearly states, "It was also said, 'Whoever divorces his wife must give her a bill of divorce.' But I say to you, whoever divorces his wife (unless the marriage is unlawful) causes her to commit adultery, and whoever marries a divorced woman commits adultery."

This teaching of Jesus may be one that sounds hard to our modern ears, but we have to strive to follow it as best we can.

However, the idea that this teaching from our Lord is a command to stay in a relationship even when things are unsafe for one of the partners or the children is a dangerous one. In fact, the Catholic Church doesn't teach that we have to stay in marriages no matter what. Canon 1153 of the *Code of Canon Law* states, "A spouse who occasions grave danger of soul or body to the other or to the children, or otherwise makes the common life unduly difficult, provides the other spouse with a reason to leave, either by a decree of the local ordinary [i.e., bishop] or, if there is danger in delay, even on his or her own authority." We're left to balance the words of Christ and the teaching of the Church and apply both to our own lives and circumstances when making the best decisions for ourselves and our family. So, we can agree with the Church when it teaches that "*divorce* is a grave offense against the natural law. It claims to break the contract, to which the spouses freely consented, to live with each other till death" (*CCC*, 2384), while we affirm that abusive relationships are not something God wants us to be a part of and that the Church provides a path for those who need to get out in order to maintain safety.

There's More to Abuse than Physical Aggression

"Some people are being seriously abused in relationships, but what's happening to me isn't *that* bad." Sadly, this is an all-too-common feeling among those of us who find ourselves in abusive relationships, maybe because media generally depicts abuse with bruises and broken limbs. There is more to abuse than physical aggression.

Physical abuse involves any way that one partner may make another feel unsafe. According to the domestic violence service agency REACH Beyond Domestic Violence, physical abuse can include "hitting, slapping, kicking, strangling, or physically restraining a partner against their will. It can also include driving recklessly or invading someone's physical space."[1]

Sexual abuse can involve rape, forcing a partner to engage in acts that they are not comfortable engaging in or consenting to, *and* withholding sex for the purposes of control and power. As the REACH team explains, "An abusive partner might also use sex as a means to judge their partner and assign a value—in other words, criticizing or saying that someone isn't good enough at sex, *or* that sex is the only thing they're good for."[2]

Verbal and emotional abuse in part involves one partner using words to cut another down, almost using words as physical blows. They are negative and nasty lies, and after hearing them repeatedly, the victim can start to believe statements such as "You're worthless," "You're ugly," or "You'll never be able to find another partner," which traps them in the unhealthy relationship. Too often people will brush off this form of abuse as not that big of a deal.

Mental and psychological abuse is one we don't think of as often, but it is no less insidious than other forms of abuse. In such circumstances, the abuser engages in behaviors specifically focused on grinding down their partner's mental health. According to the REACH team, "It often involves making the victim doubt their own sanity. We've heard stories of abusers deliberately moving car keys (and in one case, the whole car!) or a purse, dimming the lights, and flat-out denying that certain things had taken place."[3] When an abuser does this to us, we can feel trapped in the relationship because the abuser makes us believe that we need them in order to stay sane and survive.

Financial and economic abuse is a serious threat to the peace of a relationship. Abusers are almost always craving power, and one way we see influence and power attained in our world is by controlling finances. Those who have access to the most money have the most power in our world, and in a relationship where one partner is desperate to have power over the other, money becomes an obvious tool for abuse. This can come from preventing one partner from having access to money, credit cards, and bank accounts or from using a partner's name and information to build up all kinds of debt. Either form of financial abuse leaves the victim feeling trapped and unable to escape.

Cultural and identity abuse is the last form of abuse and the least known that we'll touch on here. As the REACH team explains, "Cultural abuse happens when abusers use aspects of a victim's particular cultural identity to inflict suffering, or as a means of control. Not letting someone observe the dietary or dress customs of their faith, using racial slurs, threatening to 'out' someone as LGBTQ if their friends and family don't know, or isolating someone who doesn't speak the dominant language where they live—all of these are examples of cultural abuse."[4]

Our Lord and our Church want us to open our eyes to the various means that abusers will use to keep us powerless, trapped, and afraid. Whether we're looking at our own relationships or trying to help a friend who is stuck and in need, we have to consider all these various forms of abuse, how they hurt us, and how we can safely reach out for help so we can find safety and comfort as God intends it.

So What Do We Do?

While it may not feel like it, there are always things we can do to empower ourselves in an abusive relationship. They include making ourselves a priority, establishing boundaries, stopping blaming ourselves, realizing we can't fix our abusive partner, avoiding engaging abusive language or threats, building a support network, and working on an exit plan.[5]

It can be hard to make ourselves a priority, especially when we've likely been coping with our situation by trying to please our partner. However, making choices to take care of our own mental health has to be one of the first steps toward finding wellness. We can't help others if we're not taking time for self-care. Our glass will be completely empty with nothing left to give, and things won't end well.

Equally difficult and equally important is establishing boundaries. The name calling, the screaming, the physical intimidation, the throwing things around the house, the threats—the abuse must stop. It must be clearly stated that if something like that starts to happen, we will walk away and end the interaction, we will call someone to help keep us safe. Whatever it is that we're willing to do in that moment must be clearly stated and we have to be willing to follow up the boundary setting with action.

When we're in an abusive relationship, we often blame ourselves. After all, we've been fed lies about being unlovable, about needing our abusive partner to survive, and all these lies have tilted us into feeling it's our fault that the abuse is taking place. Our partner has placed the blame squarely on our shoulders, and we've been pushed into thinking it's reality. It isn't, and we have to be willing to recognize that being abusive is a choice and the person making that choice is the only one responsible. It is never the victim's fault.

Dovetailing with this idea is the fact that we can't fix our abusive partner. Sometimes we can get locked into thinking, *If only I do this* . . . or *If only I can provide my partner with this* . . . , then they will suddenly become peaceful and the abuse will end. This isn't something we can fix within the walls of our home. An abusive partner needs intensive professional help to work through these issues and develop coping skills to help them be safe in relationships moving forward.

Similar to boundary setting, we have to be willing to avoid engaging. When we engage with abusive language or threats, when we try to create peace and calm our partner down, it only pushes the cycle further and leads to it spinning back out of control. An abusive partner becomes an expert at manipulation, and engaging with them in the midst of an abusive episode will only further allow them to push us deeper into that manipulation. Instead, we have to be willing to walk away and hold those boundaries we set earlier on.

Building a support network is crucial. We have to stop keeping secrets and find someone we trust to talk to about what's going on. Having a support network not only helps us in emergency situations but also helps us to feel less isolated. Isolation is one of the main reasons we might stay in an abusive relationship. Having a strong social support network, then, becomes key to fighting isolation and thus breaking one of the tools abusive partners use to hold us down.

Lastly, we have to start working on an exit plan, even if we still hope that the relationship can change. According to Sherri Gordon, a bullying prevention expert, "If your partner, friend, or family member has no intention of changing or working on their poor choices, you will not be able to remain in the abusive relationship forever. It will eventually take a toll on you both mentally and physically. Each situation is different. So, discuss your thoughts and ideas with a trusted friend, family member, or counselor. Remember, too, that abuse often escalates when the person being abused makes a decision to leave. So, be sure you have a safety plan in place should the abuse get worse."[6]

When it all comes down to it, leaving a relationship for the sake of our mental, physical, and emotional safety and that of our children is often the endgame in abusive situations, no matter how much work we might have put in to save the relationship. To leave successfully and safely, we must make sure we have a plan. Leaving can be difficult, but when there aren't any other options left, it becomes a matter of life and death.

Is There Healing and Relief Out There?

If you find yourself in an abusive relationship, you might see leaving as wrong, "giving up" on the other person, or sinful. As a reminder, canon law makes the Church's stance clear: "A spouse who occasions grave danger of soul or body to the other or to the children, or otherwise makes the common life unduly difficult, provides the other spouse with a reason to leave."

That being said, therapy *can* help abusive partners learn how to overcome the behavior they have learned to use in relationships, provide coping skills to help with anger outbursts, and fight back against personality issues that led to them becoming abusive in the first place. However, couples therapy *is not* recommended to achieve these goals because, the National Domestic Violence Hotline outlines, "abuse is not a 'relationship problem.' Couples counseling may imply that both partners contribute to the abusive behavior, when the choice to be abusive lies solely with the abusive partner. Focusing on communication or other relationship issues distracts from the abusive behavior, and may actually reinforce it in some cases."[7]

Individual therapy for both partners is the healthier approach in abusive relationships. For abusers specifically, the recovery expert Sharie Stines explains,

> The best-known treatment for abusers is within the context of a group, with other abusers, where the focus is on promoting personal responsibility and accountability. There are four basic requirements for changing an abuser: (1) consequences; (2) accountability; (3) confrontation; and (4) education.
>
> Abusers are difficult to treat and require long-term accountability with others before any real change can occur. Many abuser programs require their members to have at least nine months of nonabusive behavior after joining an abuser recovery group, prior to entering couples counseling.[8]

The change that we need to see in order to feel safe reentering into a relationship can only be found after intensive therapeutic intervention that the abusive partner buys into and desires to get help through.

With that in mind, there is hope that we can get out of an abusive relationship, find support, find healing and safety, and move onward day by day in our lives. And with the buy-in of our partner and their true desire to change, there is an opportunity to go through a program and process for an abusive individual to find healing and peace, and learn how to be healthy in a relationship.

Such decisions and work are not easy. But with prayer, trust in God, and a support network of good people who know how to help us, we can come out the other side into a world of peace, safety, and health.

What the Bible Says about Abuse

> Beloved, let us love one another, because love is of God; everyone who loves is begotten by God and knows God. Whoever is without love does not know God, for God is love.
>
> —1 John 4:7–8

The Catholic faith, drawing its understanding from scripture, has no place for violence, especially violence within a relationship. When we think about the relationship between partners, we think about the words of St. Paul: "Husbands, love your wives, even as Christ loved the church and handed himself over for her. . . . So [also] husbands should love their wives as their own bodies. He who loves his wife loves himself. For no one hates his own flesh but rather nourishes and cherishes it, even as Christ does the church" (Eph 5:25, 28–29). While this teaching is directed at husbands, the requirement to love applies to wives too. There can be no tolerance for physical abuse, verbal abuse, mental and emotional abuse, sexual abuse, or *any* kind of abuse.

It's by drawing on that teaching that the Church makes every effort to let the faithful know that abuse provides a reason for separating ourselves and leaving for the sake of the safety of ourselves and our children. The Bible is clear that holiness and peacefulness go hand in hand, and one who is engaging in manipulative or abusive behavior is not currently on that path to holiness. That being made clear, the Bible always provides us with hope that we can find safety and peace, and that God will reach out to us and help us through the people he puts in our lives. For the abuser, the Bible provides hope that we can turn from our sinful and reckless behaviors and find peace if we truly seek it.

What the Saints Say about Abuse

> All my hopes were in the merits of my crucified Jesus, whose image I held clasped in my hands. I consecrated myself anew to Him in life and in death.
>
> —Bl. Elizabeth Canori Mora

One holy woman who knew the reality of abuse all too well is Bl. Elizabeth Canori Mora. Born in Rome in 1774, Elizabeth grew up in a wealthy family and was mostly under the care of Augustinian nuns.[9] She developed tuberculosis, was sent home from the convent, and rather than moving in the direction of a religious vocation as many had assumed, she grew closer to the man who would become her future husband, Cristoforo Mora.

After the honeymoon phase of the relationship passed, Cristoforo became increasingly cold, jealous, and angry, and Elizabeth found herself in the midst of an abusive relationship that put her and her children's safety at risk. Elizabeth focused her attention on helping her children grow in holiness and doing everything she could to provide for her family while her husband was off wasting the family's resources.

On her death bed, after all she had been through, Elizabeth's final words were focused on her hopes and prayers that her husband would eventually convert. Her prayers were answered, for "after witnessing his holy wife's holy death, Cristoforo experienced profound remorse for the anguish he had caused his family. Repenting of his sins, he amended his life, and in a turn of events that was due in no small measure to his wife's intercession, Cristoforo lived the remaining years of his life as a Franciscan priest."[10]

Bl. Elizabeth Canori Mora is waiting to use her powerful intercession to offer up prayers on behalf of everyone suffering in an abusive relationship of any kind: prayers for their safety, for a support network to gather around them, and to help them get away from the abuse and find peace and consolation; *and* prayers for abusive partners to have a conversion of heart and to get the help they so desperately need.

IN BRIEF

- The Catholic Church doesn't teach that we have to stay in marriages no matter what.
- Abuse in a relationship can be physical, sexual, verbal and emotional, mental and psychological, financial and economic, or cultural and identity.
- Some things we can realistically do within an abusive relationship: make ourselves a priority, establish boundaries, stop blaming ourselves, realize we can't fix our abusive partner, avoid engaging with abusive behavior, build a support network, and work on an exit plan.
- As the recovery expert Sharie Stines explains, "The best-known treatment for abusers is within the context of a group, with other abusers, where the focus is on promoting personal responsibility and accountability. There are four basic requirements for changing an abuser: (1) consequences; (2) accountability; (3) confrontation; and (4) education."
- With prayer, trust in God, and a support network of good people who know how to help us, we can come out the other side into a world of peace, safety, and health.

CLOSING PRAYER

> The strength of the family lies in its capacity to love and to teach how to love.
>
> —Pope Francis

GRIEF

17. HEARTBREAK

LORD, THE ONE YOU LOVE IS CRUSHED BY GRIEF

There are few experiences meant to be more exciting and filled with hope than the news of having a baby on the way. Even in the midst of poverty and other trials in life, the anticipation can be a glimmer of hope and light.

My wife and I experienced that hopeful excitement at the positive pregnancy test announcing the pending arrival of baby number four for our family. While we had been dealt a difficult blow in the past—my wife's second pregnancy was a molar pregnancy that resulted in multiple medical procedures and all kinds of fear on my part that she might not survive—we generally were still pretty positive and naive to the reality of what could go wrong during pregnancy. However, at our twenty-week appointment, the ultrasound tech's expression made it abundantly clear that something was wrong. Over the course of the next couple of days, our son was confirmed to have a diagnosis incompatible with life after birth. In this moment, my wife and I were heartbroken. We were absolutely crushed.

This powerful reaction to grief and bereavement sticks with us still. Of course, it changes over time, becoming less searing hot and more of a dull ache, but the heartbreak that overwhelms us all in the midst of grief is something we don't soon forget. How do we even begin to cope with heartbreak in a way that allows us to see hope and light beyond the pain and darkness?

Being Heartbroken Isn't Just Feeling Blue

We all feel blue from time to time. Sadness is a normal part of life, and even periods of feeling depressed can be a completely normal experience to go through. The heartbreak we experience after the loss of a loved one and the continued darkness we go through as we move through the grieving process is altogether different. According to the clinical psychologist Deborah Khoshaba, "During the first few months after a loss, many signs and symptoms of simple grief are the same as those of complicated grief, although for the latter, they linger and worsen. Complicated grief is a chronic, heightened state of mourning."[1]

We will touch on some of the symptoms of complicated grief in this section—specifically, the inability to enjoy life, trouble carrying out normal routines, and withdrawing from social activities.[2] Being heartbroken in the wake of grief and bereavement is not just being sad and missing the person who has gone on before us but rather an absolute and total devastation, an experience where we find ourselves actively praying for God to step in and end our pain in whatever means he'd like.

I remember at first praying for God to take my life and let our son live, and later praying for God to take my life just so I could be with our son again. This is the level of heartbreak we're talking about here. For me, I had a wife and three other children who needed me to stick around, not only to be there for the typical roles of husband and father but also to help the family walk through their grief. And yet I was so crushed to the depths of my soul that if God would have given me the option to check out of the pain and brokenness, I would have accepted it without a second thought.

Looking back, it's hard to even imagine how devastated I was. Even though we've all experienced death, even though we all know that we and everyone we know *will* die, it still presents itself as something unnatural, something that feels like it goes against what it means to be a child of God. And when we're in the depths of this heartbreak because of our grief and bereavement, it feels like we're never going to get back to the way we were before.

So What Do We Do?

First and foremost, we have to realize that grief and bereavement are seriously misunderstood experiences in our world. We can see it when friends and family members offer us platitudes in our grief in an effort to help us feel better. Most things we hear are just efforts to cut through the discomfort others have in standing alongside our intense pain, but platitudes show us that most of us lack a real understanding of what grief is. Grief won't go away if we ignore it, and how we show or don't show our grief has no indication on whether we're "really" grieving. There is no time frame in which we can expect our grief to subside; we don't need to be strong in the face of loss; and moving on means that we've come to accept our loss, not that we no longer feel it.

Platitudes often come out of myths related to grieving, and learning to separate the myths from reality when it comes to our grief is a great first step toward healing. When we learn the realities, we start to feel validated and see that our experience may be much more normal than we realize. This validation helps us see that there are other people out there who have been just as heartbroken as we are. We aren't alone. Those people, putting one foot in front of the other, day by day, give us hope that we will also be able to move through the grief process, no matter how difficult, one step at a time.

An important guideline when we're heartbroken and grieving: "Don't let anyone tell you how to feel, and don't tell yourself how to feel either."[3] Let yourself feel whatever you feel without judgment. We have to cut ourselves some slack and allow ourselves and the people grieving alongside us to experience grief as it comes and acknowledge that however it affects us is okay. There is no "right way" to feel when you're brokenhearted and crushed from grief.

Is There Healing and Relief Out There?

Of course, there's a big difference between having insight that you should be able to feel whatever you feel as you go through the grief process without judgment, embarrassment, or a timeline and actually feeling better. While the insight can be an immensely helpful first step, it's just the beginning of our progress.

Some initial steps to push forward step by step through the grief process are

- accept your feelings;
- recognize that grieving is a process that takes time;
- embrace the current moment rather than focusing on the past or future;
- connect with loved ones;
- take time to care for yourself;
- acknowledge that special times of the year will bring back memories, and make traditions and new memories in honor of that;
- seek a support group; and
- get professional help from a therapist.[4]

Focusing on the heartbreak we experience in the bereavement process, I'd like to go a bit deeper on the ideas of rest and rejuvenation, special times of year, and support groups.

Getting the right amount of rest is one of the primary preventative coping skills for most mental health situations. Those of us who have experienced depression, anxiety, mood disorders, or serious grief and bereavement can almost always take a look at our sleeping patterns and see a correlation between bad sleep and an upswing in the other symptoms we've been experiencing.

That being said, one of the most common symptoms that cuts across all mental health experiences is difficulty sleeping. All we can do is try our best to set ourselves up to get a good night's sleep. That involves doing things that help tell our brain we're going to be powering down for the night, such as turning off screens (especially in bed), having something soothing to drink (such as decaffeinated tea), and maybe doing something low energy that brings us peace (such as praying).

Planning ahead for those special times of the year is crucial if we want to be ready to cope with triggering dates in a healthy manner. Birthdays, holidays, the day our loved one died: these are all times of the year that are potentially emotionally triggering, and if we let them descend upon us without taking the time to prepare for how we're going to handle them, our heart will be broken open all over again. We have to prepare for the hard times when we're feeling okay.

For example, during easier periods in the grief process, we can write down what we're going to do when a hard day comes, specifically when an anniversary or holiday pops up on the calendar. That way, when we're having a hard day or preparing for a special time of year, we can pull out the list of ideas, coping skills, and ways of remembering or honoring our loved one and use those to mark the day.

Finally, we need to come to realize the value of a support group. This group can be a therapeutic one our doctor or local community agency refers us to. For most of us, though, we simply need to be willing to share our heartbreak and grief with someone we trust. We have to be willing to put ourselves out there and find a community that knows what it's like to go through the experience we're trying to navigate.

Our heartbreak tries to get us to buy into the lie that no one can possibly understand what we're going through, but it's just simply not true. Sure, most people don't know what it's like to lose a child. And those trying to provide comfort often end up saying something so wrong, so hurtful, and so bizarre for the situation that they only drive home the idea that most people don't understand what it's like. But guess what? I'm here, my wife is here, and loads of other people are around you, and we know precisely what it feels like. The same is true for other heartbreaking losses. There are people unafraid to hear you talk about the deep and dark emotions and thoughts you're experiencing because they've had those exact same deep and dark emotions and thoughts. But we won't be able to find each other unless we allow ourselves to become vulnerable and share our pain with people we trust. It's hard, but it's so crucial.

What the Bible Says about Heartbreak

> He will wipe every tear from their eyes, and there shall be no more death or mourning, wailing or pain, [for] the old order has passed away.
>
> —Revelation 21:4

I go back to two words in the Gospel of John more than any others: "Jesus wept" (Jn 11:35). When I find myself in the midst of intense grieving, even now as I sit years on the other side of my darkest hour, I look to those words to feel close to God, to feel his presence in the midst of my pain. It's powerful to know that Jesus wept over the death of a friend, that he was deeply troubled because of his grief.

Jesus—who knew better than any of us that God the Father can bring good out of suffering, death in this life does not have the final word, every tear will be wiped away from our eyes, and death and suffering will be no more—wept. He wept just like us. He cried over the death of a loved one in the same way we do. It's one of the most profound and beautiful insights in the gospel.

That being said, scripture offers us more than the knowledge that Jesus also experienced grief. Over and over again we hear the message that all of our pain, suffering, and heartbreak will be healed when Christ welcomes us into his kingdom. This message is especially important for all of us walking through the grief process: "But I will see you again, and your hearts will rejoice, and no one will take your joy away from you" (Jn 16:22).

This life presents us with many moments where our joy is stolen from us. But Christ offers us healing and the answer to all of our suffering. And once we're with him, our joy will never be taken away again. But for now, as we walk through this dark valley waiting hopefully for Christ to free us from death and mourning and save us even though we have been crushed in spirit, we can open up and allow ourselves to weep as our Lord did, to feel connected to him, and to pick up the pieces of our shattered hearts in order to move forward and find peace.

What the Saints Say about Heartbreak

> When I had to close the eyes of my dear little children and bury them, I felt great sorry, but I was always resigned to it. I did not regret the pains and the sorrows which I had endured for them. . . . I don't think that the sorrows and the troubles endured could possibly be compared with the

> eternal happiness of my children with God. Besides, they are not lost to me forever.
>
> —St. Zélie Martin

There's a popular misunderstanding in our Catholic world that the closer we come to Christ and the more willing we are to work on our spiritual lives, the better our lives will be. This is one of the most dangerous lies we hear. I mean, just look at what happened to Jesus, look at what happened to his Blessed Mother, and look at what happened to his friends!

We can also look at St. Zélie Martin, who was no stranger to the absolute heartbreak that comes from grief. Born two days before Christmas in 1831 in France, Marie-Azélie "Zélie" Guérin Martin would go on to become one of the most famous parents in the history of the Catholic Church. Her daughter is the much loved St. Thérèse of Lisieux, but it's her experience of child loss and her reaction to that loss that drew me closer to her.

Zélie was the mother to nine children in all: five daughters who would go on to find vocations as religious sisters and four who would go on to their eternal life far too soon. Three of her children died before reaching their first birthday, and the other passed away at the age of five.

We get some of her thoughts on the heartbreak from a letter she wrote to her sister, who suffered a miscarriage and felt as heartbroken as Zélie herself:

> When I had to close the eyes of my dear children and bury them, I felt deep sorrow, but I was always resigned to it. I did not regret the pains and the sorrows which I had endured for them. Many persons said to me: "It would have been better for you if you had never had them." I could not bear that kind of talk. I do not think that the sorrows and the troubles endured could possibly be compared with the eternal happiness of my children with God. Besides, they are not lost to me forever; life is short and filled with crosses, and we shall find them again in Heaven. Above all, it was on the death of my first child that I felt more deeply the happiness of having a child in Heaven, for God showed me in a noticeable way that He

> accepted my sacrifice. Through the intercession of my little angel, I received a very extraordinary grace.[5]

Would that all of us, in the midst of our own heartbreak brought on by grief and bereavement, see things in the same way as St. Zélie Martin. Thankfully, she's waiting for us to ask her to intercede on our behalf for just that purpose.

IN BRIEF

- Heartbreak can crush us to the depths of our soul. In my darkest grief, if God would have given me the option to check out of the pain and brokenness, I would have accepted it without a second thought.
- Learning to separate the myths from reality when it comes to our grief is a great first step toward healing. When we learn the realities, we start to feel validated and see that our experience may be much more normal than we think it is.
- Planning ahead for those special times of the year is crucial if we want to be ready to cope with triggering dates in a healthy manner.
- Our heartbreak tries to get us to buy into the lie that no one can possibly understand what we're going through, but it is simply not true.
- "Jesus wept" (Jn 16:22). Jesus understands our grief because he experienced grief. Scripture offers the answer to all of our suffering: over and over again we hear the message that all of our pain, suffering, and heartbreak will be healed when Christ welcomes us into his kingdom.

CLOSING PRAYER

> Eternal Father, I offer you the most precious blood of your divine Son, Jesus, in union with the masses said throughout the world today, for all the holy souls in purgatory, for sinners everywhere,

for sinners in the universal church, those in my own home and within my family. Amen. Jesus, Jesus, Jesus.

—Prayer of St. Gertrude for the Souls in Purgatory

18. JOYLESSNESS

LORD, THE ONE YOU LOVE DOESN'T EVEN WANT TO FEEL BETTER

There are few feelings like being absolutely joyless. We covered the idea of anhedonia in chapter 1, but even that doesn't quite capture the experience of joylessness that comes in the midst of grief and bereavement. From the moment our son was diagnosed with a prenatal condition incompatible with life, through the rest of his time with us and after the blessed hour we got to spend with him in the labor and delivery unit at the hospital, I felt as though I had crossed this threshold into a new life, one of bitterness and torment, tears and anger, where there would never again be any reason to feel joy.

In all honesty, I didn't want to. My grief was so intense that even the thought of joy made me feel ashamed. I felt as though the rest of my life was going to be miserable, and *it needed to be miserable* for me to adequately honor the intensity of my son's short life and death.

It's shocking when I look back and think about that feeling that swirled around me at the time. It took *a long* time for me to be able to experience brief moments of joy without feeling immediately guilty and ashamed, and from time to time I still feel as though I don't deserve happiness. In my situation, however, it was our other children who pushed me out of this aspect of my grief, almost forcing me to engage in those joyful moments with them. If it weren't for them, I would have wallowed in my joylessness forever, and I owe them all my gratitude for basically saving my life with their own beautiful sense of unstoppable joy.

If it weren't for them, who knows where I would have ended up. Because let me tell you, the joyless feeling that assaults us when we're trying to survive intense grief feels as if it could literally end up being a killer if left unaddressed.

Joylessness Isn't Just Apathy

When I say "joylessness" in the context of grief, I'm referring to an absolute inability to feel any joy whatsoever. It's an overwhelming feeling that we no longer deserve to experience joy, and if we get even the smallest glimmer of joy, we feel we're betraying the loved one we've lost. In joylessness, we conclude that *we will never experience joy ever again* and that maybe that's what we deserve.

This overwhelming joylessness after the loss of a loved one may be connected to the way our memory operates in the midst of grief. Some research shows that our grieving brain may start to become fuzzy in terms of our memories, with the exception of memories of the person we lost. According to Harvard University researchers Donald Robinaugh and Richard McNally, the "same brain mechanism that controls autobiographical memory also controls visions of the future," and psychological scientists studying grief and memory discovered that mourners who experienced extreme joylessness "had clear defects of both memory and imagination. They were unable to recall specific events from the past, nor could they conjure up detailed future scenarios. . . . This cognitive deficit was apparent only when the events did not include the deceased. When recalling past events with their partner—or projecting future events—these extreme mourners were no different" than other mourners who had experienced less extreme grief.[1]

Here we see a reason for our joylessness. Our bereaved brain is impaired at retrieving past memories or thinking of future experiences we might have but are very clearly focused on our deceased loved one, thus compounding our pain and sorrow in addition to amplifying our hopelessness.

With all this collapsing down on top of us, we become overwhelmed by joylessness and certain that the joy of our past life will never return.

So What Do We Do?

We have to double down on remembering that everyone's grief process looks and lasts differently, and that's okay. Our ability to cope with the joylessness we experience may come later than another's, and that's all a part of grief and loss. We have to be willing to accept this. Putting constraints on ourselves or allowing the artificial constraints of others to get into our mind is only going to cause us deeper despair and make our movement through the grief process more difficult.

With that in mind, there are definitely things we can do to move toward coping with that joylessness: talk about the death of our loved one, accept our feelings, take care of ourselves, and reach out to others.[2]

We've covered accepting our feelings in a previous chapter, so here we'll focus on talking about the death of our loved one (which is related to reaching out to others with their loss) and taking care of ourselves.

When we're going through the grief process, our initial response is to push everyone away and shut down our social communication. As we explored earlier, this is connected to our idea that no one can possibly understand what we're going through. The avoidance, however, compounds our loneliness and keeps that valuable social support system at a distance. We have to push through what our brain is telling us is best and remember that opening up and allowing ourselves to be vulnerable with those whom we can trust has the potential to help us.

Talking about our grief is one of our best tools for coping. When we open ourselves up to share our story, we create the opportunity to impact the lives of others going through a similar experience. This is powerful. This ability to transform our loss and resulting joylessness into something productive, meaningful, and helpful to others is transformational and can become a crucial stepping-stone toward recovering that sense of joy, hope, and meaning about our own life.

Taking care of ourselves, the next big coping skill, can sometimes feel impossible. When we're weighed down by joylessness, taking care of ourselves seems pointless. Our joyless grieving brain absolutely fights against the impulse to take care of ourselves. And yet we know that taking care of ourselves—eating well, exercising, practicing good hygiene, and sleeping well—helps to elevate our mood even when everything else is a struggle.

When we're joyless from grief, sometimes we have to go through the motions, take one step at a time, and hope that something—*anything*—will give us a small taste of that emotion we feel we've lost forever. Taking care of ourselves, even in as small and seemingly insignificant ways as brushing our teeth or leaving the house to get the mail, can be that step.

Is There Healing and Relief Out There?

When we're stuck inside this cycle of grief, joylessness, and hopelessness, we can often feel as though there's no relief in sight. Similar to the lie our brain tells us that we don't deserve to ever feel joy again, we experience the lie that we will never, ever feel better. Thankfully, in addition to the coping skills noted above, there is developing evidence that a few different therapeutic techniques offer relief in our grief process.

First, there doesn't have to be some threshold where our grief is bad enough or lasts long enough before we seek professional help. Quite the opposite, actually, as the best approach to working through our grief is tackling it as early as we feel possible. It's never a bad idea to reach out to a therapist or doctor who might be able to offer some relief as we move through the process at our own pace.

By working with a therapist through our complicated grief, we may

- learn about complicated grief and how it's treated;
- explore such topics as grief reactions, complicated grief symptoms, adjusting to our loss, and redefining our life goals;
- hold imagined conversations with our loved one and retell the circumstances of the death to help us become less distressed by images and thoughts of our loved one;
- explore and process thoughts and emotions;
- improve coping skills; and
- reduce feelings of blame and guilt.[3]

According to the clinical social worker and educator Dr. Kim Glickman, this kind of therapy can help us adapt "to the loss by keeping grief center stage, honoring the person who died, and envisioning a future with possibilities for happiness."[4]

In addition to therapy focused on grief and bereavement, we may need the additional help of medication, even if only temporarily. Study after study shows that the most effective mental health treatment is the combination of medication and therapy, as we often need the push from the medication to find the motivation and energy to work on the therapeutic tasks that will help carry us forward toward finding wellness.

What the Bible Says about Joylessness

> The righteous cry out, the LORD hears
> and he rescues them from all their afflictions.
> The LORD is close to the brokenhearted,
> saves those whose spirit is crushed.
>
> —Psalm 34:18–19

Reflecting on joylessness leads me to focus on these words of Christ: "So you also are now in anguish. But I will see you again, and your hearts will rejoice, and no one will take your joy away from you" (Jn 16:22). When I read these words and hold them up alongside other words from scripture, I feel hope in my joylessness, but that hope is not in the present moment being turned into one without suffering. Far from it.

In all honesty, if I take away one thought from scripture related to my grief and joylessness, it's that Jesus will eventually wipe away every tear. He will eventually restore our joy and never allow it to be taken away. He will welcome us into a place where none of the hardships and suffering we experience in our present lives will continue, where we will be free from the heartbreak of loss. But that place isn't necessarily going to be in the here and now.

That's a really hard message to balance: the hope that every suffering will end but the realization that it may not end here and now. It's the difficult balance of believing that God can perform miracles in our lives but also recognizing that miracles may not arrive in the way that we expect or want them to. Referring to the son she lost and what he meant for her in her life, Servant of God Chiara Corbella Petrillo said, "He demonstrated that God performs miracles, but not with our logical limitations, because God is something greater than our desires (he knocked down the idea of those who seek not salvation of the soul in God but only that of the body; of all those who ask God for a happy and simple life that does not at all resemble the life of the cross that Jesus left us)."[5]

This represents the deeper message that we have a hard time grasping, especially in the midst of grief and joylessness. As Isaiah 55:8–9 says, "For my thoughts are not your thoughts, nor are your ways my ways—oracle of the LORD. For as the heavens are higher than the earth, so are my ways higher than your ways, my thoughts higher than your thoughts." When we pray and beg for God to deliver us from our suffering, free us from our joylessness, he *will* respond. But because we allow ourselves to be limited to what we can experience with our senses and struggle to see everything else there is to our reality, we fail to grasp *how* he does this.

Those of us crushed under the weight of grief, brokenhearted seemingly beyond repair, can be sure that the Lord will save us; we can be sure that he will keep that promise. We just have to remember to be open to the possibility that this saving will come to us at a time and a place and in a way that we don't expect.

What the Saints Say about Joylessness

> In every disappointment let your heart fly directly to your dear Savior. Jesus will never leave you or forsake you.
>
> —St. Elizabeth Ann Seton

Many of the saints experienced joylessness, grief, and heartbreak and yet they had something that gave them the strength to carry on through the darkness.

St. Elizabeth Ann Seton was one of those saints. Born in New York City in 1774, Elizabeth knew grief and heartbreak. Her mother died when Elizabeth was just three years old. Her baby sister, whose birth may have led to the death of her mother, died the following year.

Elizabeth's father remarried, and her stepmother was a kind and considerate person in Elizabeth's life. The marriage ended in divorce, however, at which point Elizabeth lost her "second mother" and went through a dark time of grieving.

At the age of nineteen, she married a wealthy businessman and had five children. But her life would be turned upside down again, as he died just nine years into their marriage, leaving Elizabeth alone to raise the children and support the family. She had traveled to Italy at the time of his passing, as that's where he was when he died, and discovered the Catholic faith. Somehow, in the midst of her grief, she was inspired to convert to Catholicism. She then moved in 1809 to Emmitsburg, Maryland, where she founded the Sisters of Charity of St. Joseph's, the first community for religious women established in the United States. She also began St. Joseph's Academy and Free School, planting the seeds of Catholic education in the United States."[6] Life after conversion and becoming a founder wasn't much easier, however. She struggled with misunderstandings and interpersonal conflicts and continued to deal with loss with the deaths of two her daughters, other loved ones, and young sisters in her community.

We can look to St. Elizabeth Ann Seton when we want to see an example of someone who faced heartbreak after heartbreak, someone who experienced the deep and dark joylessness associated with grief and mourning, and yet someone who pushed forward in spite of it all. By learning more about Mother Seton, may we all feel the grace of God working in the darkness of our lives and grow closer to Elizabeth, someone who is ready to intercede for relief from our joylessness, at the same time.

IN BRIEF

- In joylessness, we conclude that *we will never experience joy ever again*, and that maybe that's what we deserve.
- There is a reason for our joylessness. Our bereaved brain is impaired at retrieving past memories or thinking of future experiences we might have but are very clearly focused on our deceased loved one, thus compounding our pain and sorrow in addition to amplifying our hopelessness.

- We have to remember that everyone's grief process looks and lasts differently, and that's okay. Our ability to cope with joylessness may come later than another's, and that's all part of grief and loss.
- We can start to get help by talking about our grief and by taking care of ourselves, even when we don't want to do either.
- Thankfully, there is developing evidence that a few different therapeutic techniques offer relief in our grief process, including talk therapy and medication.

CLOSING PRAYER

O holy St. Philip Neri, patron saint of joy, you who trusted scripture's promise that the Lord is always at hand and that we need not have anxiety about anything, in your compassion heal our worries and sorrows and lift the burdens from our hearts. We come to you as one whose heart swells with abundant love for God and all creation. Hear us, we pray, especially in this need [*make your request here*]. Keep us safe through your loving intercession, and may the joy of the Holy Spirit that filled your heart, St. Philip, transform our lives and bring us peace. Amen.

—Prayer to St. Philip Neri

19. POWERLESSNESS

LORD, THE ONE YOU LOVE FEELS WEAK

As my wife and I received the devastating news about our son's diagnosis, I desperately wanted to do something to fix what was going wrong. Eventually I turned to God and prayed for a miracle, for the diagnosis to be incorrect, for God to take my life in order to spare my son's.

After our son's birth and death, my mind turned to other ideas of creating a sense of control in our lives. I made sure to keep our other kids close to me at all times, watching them like a hawk, ensuring that they'd not be getting involved in *anything* that might hurt them. Despite my best effort, I was powerless over the result of my trauma, continually envisioning the death of our other children in my mind as a residue of sorts from the loss of our baby.

All of us experience these times in our lives where we realize we lack control. Something happens that forces us to recognize that we ultimately don't have any power over our lives and the lives of those around us. We can do absolutely everything to keep our family free from harm, we can make all the right choices, and yet it still comes.

Our Catholic faith says that God allows certain trials into our lives for the purpose of reminding us that ultimately we have no choice but to trust in him. He is in control, and we are not. This doesn't happen for an evil purpose. God knows that the key to having a life of peace, joy, and holiness is learning to rely totally on him. Yet for better or worse, we tend not to rely totally on him until everything we hold dear has been stripped away. In the case of my family, it was the veil being pulled back on the experience of having a child, believing that he "belonged" to us, and wanting to parent him in the way we wanted to parent him. In the moment, I wouldn't have been able to hear this, but years removed from the searing-hot pain of loss, I'm able to recognize that God was able to bring good out of our suffering: a realization of our absolute dependence on God and our refreshed desire to grow in holiness and follow him to heaven so we can hold our baby once more.

The Catholic faith is full of dichotomies: a servant leader, a baby who is truly God, the idea that when we are weak we are strong. In this case, it is when we realize we are powerless that we are actually able to be powerful. I wish it didn't have to be that way. I wish that I could have found the desire to grow in holiness and rely totally on God without the loss of my child. Instead, I felt the deflating and terrifying feeling of powerlessness in the midst of grief, and it's something I carry with me every day.

Powerlessness Isn't Just Feeling Weak

When we face a moment of tremendous suffering in our lives, it's natural and normal to feel weak. Powerlessness in the face of grief, however, is a far more overwhelming and intense experience. It is the feeling that what we once understood about our abilities, our role in life, and even our opportunities to receive anything good from God have all been ripped away.

As a husband and father, I have long envisioned that one of the roles God has in store for my life is to protect and lead my family, to keep my children and wife as free from harm as I can, and to help them see the beauty and goodness in the world. When we walked through the death of our son, however, all of that was torn away from me in an instant. I was left feeling completely powerless, without a true understanding of what my purpose in life was. I no longer felt as though I had the ability to protect my children, to guide my family, or to help them see that the world is a good and beautiful place. Instead, I could do nothing to help save my son, nothing to keep my other children and wife from heartbreak and suffering, nothing to help them understand the why behind suffering that seems so pointless, and nothing to show them that goodness and beauty existed in a world where to me it felt like it no longer did.

Powerlessness is a terrible, all-encompassing feeling that destroys us from the inside. We lose our ability to maintain our regular patterns or maintain any semblance of our routine. Our entire world is rocked. And that sense of powerlessness in light of our grief starts to bleed into other areas of our life. We start to feel powerless at work, among friends, in the Church, everywhere. It wears us down; it brings us to our knees and leads to a feeling of hopelessness that starts to overshadow every aspect of our being.

So What Do We Do?

In 2 Corinthians 12:10, St. Paul lays out our basic premise here: "For when I am weak, then I am strong." When we are facing the feeling of being weak and powerless in the grief journey, we can actually come to a point where we start to understand that it is in our weakness that we can find our greatest strength, a strength that we have through God.

God sees everything. He knows how every little piece of our lives fits together. He knows the good that can come from suffering. He understands how something we want to avoid may actually be the exact thing that leads us to growing in holiness, to bringing our family closer to the path headed for heaven. We can all eventually come to the realization that all of the experiences in our lives (good, bad, and in the middle) make us who we are, both in this world and on into the next. God sees all of this, but we don't, so our first step is to trust him, even when it feels awful and unfair to do so.

Another way to describe this powerlessness we feel is "floundering":

> Trust yourself to flounder. After all, your world has been turned upside down. The previous order of your life has become totally disordered. Floundering is the correct and logical result. Trust it. Perhaps we cannot make decisions or complete tasks because this is not the best time to make decisions or attempt tasks. Have faith that your new version of life will unfold, however slowly, and the course of your future will be revealed. Give it time and trust yourself to

> understand what to do and when to do it. Don't rush it or force it. Be patient and kind to yourself.[1]

Yes, we feel powerless in the wake of an experience that has left us reeling from grief. That feeling of being powerless is normal. We have to cut ourselves some slack, not put a timeline on our grief process, and give ourselves a break for all the difficult emotions we experience. They hurt, but they are normal and no one (including ourselves) should suggest otherwise.

Trusting God and then trusting ourselves and our process are the keys to starting our journey of coping with feeling powerless.

Is There Healing and Relief Out There?

The healing and relief that we might find in the wake of feeling powerless because of our grief will not be in suddenly feeling powerful again. Instead, it will come from figuring out how to accept, respect, and live with the knowledge that we are powerless and we only have strength and power through our Lord. Our weakness helps us to understand this.

With all that being said, there are ways that we can ease our journey through this grief process and through the understanding of our powerlessness. Some coping mechanisms that can help us "honor the grief surrounding" us and lead us down that path of healing and relief include the following:

- Bear witness and communicate. Sharing our stories is an essential step, [trauma counselor Terri] Daniel says. "If you can't talk about what's happened to you and you can't share it, you can't really start working on it. So, communicate with your friends and family about your experience."
- Write, create, express. Whether you're an extrovert or introvert, keeping a written or recorded journal of these days offers another way to express, to identify and to acknowledge loss and grief.
- Meditate. Regular meditation and just taking time to slow down and take several deep, calming breaths throughout the day also works to lower stress and is available to everyone.

- Be open to joy. And finally . . . make sure to let joy and gratitude into your life during these challenging times.[2]

These are great first steps when tackling the experience of being overwhelmed with feeling powerless in the midst of any kind of grief.

If there's one theme present throughout this part on grief, it is the idea of sharing our story. Bearing witness to what we're going through, allowing ourselves to be open and vulnerable with others when it's safe, telling our story for the sake of our own healing, and opening ourselves up to helping others are keys to wellness in the face of grief. It also may help another who is going through the same experience, and *that* is the power that we find in our weakness and the hope we find in our darkest moment.

What the Bible Says about Feeling Powerless

> We are powerless before this vast multitude that is coming against us. We ourselves do not know what to do, so our eyes are turned toward you.
>
> —2 Chronicles 20:12

St. Paul's words "For when I am weak, then I am strong" (2 Cor 12:10) articulate the key to our hope in our powerlessness. It's a mystery, a difficult-to-accept teaching of our Lord, and yet it gives us the map for conceptualizing and understanding everything about our suffering and our moments of weakness.

There's a quote attributed to St. Teresa of Calcutta that helps me understand and accept this teaching: "We must empty ourselves so that God can fill us." None of us wants to be emptied out; it goes against our selfish human nature. And so I would never choose to empty myself out, even if I knew that God would fill that emptiness with something beyond my wildest dreams, with himself. And because of that, God permits moments where we can't help but be emptied out, moments where we can't help but find ourselves weak and powerless. These moments hurt, and they don't feel fair. Yet they teach us something we can't learn any other way: there is no answer to the questions we have in our lives except the answer of falling into the arms of God and relying totally on him.

We look at our lives, suffering, and grief and we can't help but join with Job as he calls out, "What strength have I that I should endure?" (Jb 6:11), and we find the answer that comes from 2 Chronicles: "We ourselves do not know what to do, *so our eyes are turned toward you*" (20:12; emphasis added).

What the Saints Say about Feeling Powerless

> I thank God that my Goliath is finally dead and that my eyes are free to look beyond and to follow God without having fear of being what I am.
>
> —Servant of God Chiara Corbella Petrillo

Servant of God Chiara Corbella Petrillo was someone who realized that we find our strength in our weakness, we find our power in our moments of powerlessness, and we find our hope and salvation in those times where all seems dark and lost, and she willingly allowed herself to be powerless in light of that realization.

Chiara Corbella Petrillo was born in 1984 in Rome, the younger of two children. Her life would be set off in a direction she didn't even expect in the summer of 2002 while visiting Medjugorje with some classmates. She met her future husband there, and the pair would marry at the San Pietro church in Assisi in 2008.

One month after their wedding, they discovered they were expecting, but their excitement at the news was dashed when an ultrasound showed that their unborn daughter was diagnosed with anencephaly. Their daughter, Maria Grazia Letizia, was born on June 10, 2009, and died within about a half hour. The couple became pregnant again, and unbelievably, the ultrasound for their second child showed that their son developed without kidneys. Because of not having kidneys, there was a lack of fluid in the uterus that led to the baby not being able to fully develop his lungs before birth. On June 24, 2010, Davide Giovanni was born, baptized, given all the love the couple could give, and died within thirty-eight minutes.

The couple became pregnant again, and this time the ultrasound showed that the baby was completely healthy. And yet, instead of having an opportunity to rejoice, they were faced with more pain as Chiara was diagnosed with carcinoma after finding a lesion on her tongue. Their third child, Francisco, was born on May 30, 2011, and this carcinoma would continue to worsen, leading to Charia's death on June 13, 2012.

Servant of God Chiara Corbella Petrillo, and her witness in the midst of intense grief, sorrow, and feelings of being absolutely powerless, yet finding strength in Christ and his love in the middle of it all, inspires me every single day. After Davide's death in 2010, Chiara wrote, "Who is Davide? A little one who received as a gift from God a very important role: that of knocking down the great Goliaths that are inside each one of us—knocking down our power as parents as we make decisions about him and for him. He shows us that he would grow and that he was like this because God has need of him like this."[3] With her words and actions, she shows us how to embrace the life God gives us with joy and a willingness to be powerless for our Lord.

She shows us what we need to know in order to follow God through the dark valleys, and for that I will be forever grateful.

IN BRIEF

- God allows certain trials into our lives to remind us that ultimately we have no choice but to trust in him. He is in control, and we are not.
- When we face a tremendous moment of suffering in our lives, it's natural and normal to feel weak. Powerlessness in the face of grief, however, is a far more overwhelming and intense experience—the feeling that what we once understood about our abilities, our role in the life of our family, and even our opportunities to receive anything good from God have all been ripped away.
- All of the experiences in our life (good, bad, and in the middle) make us who we are, both in this world and into the next, and from God's vantage point that can all be seen. We cannot see that, which is why our first step is to trust him even when it feels awful and unfair to do so.
- Bearing witness to what we're going through, allowing ourselves to be open and vulnerable with others when it's safe, and telling

our story for the sake of our own healing and others' healing are keys to wellness in the face of grief.

CLOSING PRAYER

> Simply surrender to the power of God's love, which is always greater than our weakness.
>
> —St. Francis de Sales

20. SUBSTANCE ABUSE

LORD, THE ONE YOU LOVE IS SELF-MEDICATING

As I carried my final belongings from the car to the dorm room and my parents began to say their goodbyes to their newly minted college boy, my mom gave me one last piece of advice: "Remember, alcoholism runs in your birth family, so don't even think about it." As an adopted child, I'd heard many such comments from my mother through the years, but this advice didn't come strictly out of her concern for what might happen to me if I gave into a life of partying too hard away from home. For her, it was much more personal than that.

My mother grew up in a big family. One thing that seemed to plague some of her family was a penchant for drinking. My mother had seen it all, as a child and as a young adult, and because of what she experienced within her family she decided not to drink alcohol at all. I can't remember a single time I saw my mother drinking. The closest she came to it was a virgin strawberry daiquiri on a cruise back in the '90s.

While her influence didn't keep me from spending some of my college days in a haze that can only be produced by the cheapest beer possible, it did plant a seed in my mind of what alcohol and other substances have the potential to do: destroy lives, end careers, rip apart families, estrange children from their parents, allow behavior that would otherwise be unthinkable, and take life.

The purpose of this chapter is not to make the claim that we need to abstain from alcohol under any circumstances lest we find ourselves alone and eventually six feet under. Rather, it is to look into why substance use can be a problem for some of us and not for others, to bring awareness to the interactions between our mental health and our substance use, and to explore a better path forward for coping with our emotional difficulties and life circumstances.

I've asked myself, *Why am I able to consume some substances and be able to go on with my life without it taking over, while my good friend does the same but ends up going down a dark path that leads to so much loss, pain, and suffering?*

This brings us to a realization that helps us have compassion toward our sisters and brothers suffering from substance use issues *and* to have the right frame of mind when considering what would be helpful in our families and in the world at large.

Substance Use Disorders Are Not Anyone's Fault

Substance use disorders are not the fault of the individual suffering or the fault of any loved ones suffering alongside them. This can often be a difficult truth to accept, because our attitudes toward those who engage in problematic substance use are tied up in our emotions, relationships, and pain. Most of us feel it would just be easier if we could pin the blame on someone or something. After all, if we or someone we love is abusing substances, the negative impact of that abuse hits all of us, and we really don't know how to conceptualize the situation in a healthy manner.

A person suffering from chronic and severe mental illness will make choices that they wouldn't normally make under healthier circumstances, and those of us caught up in substance abuse are in the same boat. We steal, break relationships, lose jobs, drop out of school, get involved in the criminal justice system, and even hurt our closest loved ones just to get what we think we need. And when our loved ones let us know how much we're hurting them, we see them as trying to stop us from getting what we know we need, and slowly but surely everything falls apart. We suffer in this way because addiction is a disease. According to the National Institute on Drug Abuse (NIDA), "A disease is a condition that changes the way an organ functions. Addiction does this to the brain, changing the brain on a physiological level. It literally alters the way the brain works, rewiring its fundamental structure."[1] Understanding this helps us to better understand how to help loved ones. They need treatment; just stopping most likely isn't going to be the answer.

Drugs trigger the part of our brain that releases dopamine, which lets us feel pleasure. Drug use initially releases greater amounts of dopamine than activities such as exercise or eating do, which is how people become addicted. However, "over time, drug use leads to much smaller releases of dopamine. That means the brain's reward center is less receptive to pleasure and enjoyment, both from drugs as well as from everyday sources like relationships or activities that a person once enjoyed. Once the brain has been altered by drug use, it requires more and more drugs just to function at a baseline level."[2]

It might be helpful to imagine a world where everything looked like an old black-and-white television show, every meal tasted like boiled cabbage, and every relationship felt no different from ones with acquaintances you barely have anything in common with. An entire life with a subpar amount of pleasure, everything just feeling kind of "bleh." This could be because of untreated depression, or it could be because of an all-consuming grief or other pain. And then you come into contact with a substance that turns the world around you to the brightest rainbow of colors you've ever seen, makes every meal taste like the best thing that's ever been prepared, and your relationships become explosions of love and connection that you never imagined possible.

It feels great, and you would do absolutely anything to get that feeling again. The more of this substance you use, the more it takes to get you back to that same feeling, but it never quite gets you to that same level of pleasure you experienced the first time around. Eventually you find you have to use this substance just to get yourself back to that old feeling of black-and-white TV, bland and flavorless food, and ho-hum relationships, because at least when you were feeling that way you could still semi-function.

Substance use is a disease that literally changes the way our brain functions and must be treated as such. We shouldn't blame someone for their brain chemistry or lack of dopamine being released at normal everyday pleasures any more than we should blame someone for developing type-1 diabetes, for example, or any other chronic condition caused by their biology.

So What Do We Do?

First and foremost, we have to seek out the help of someone who can guide us in getting treatment for our dependence issues. This doesn't necessarily mean that we must find a professional. We might find help from people practicing sobriety at a local support group or from a hotline that can provide us information and referrals to support services specific to our substance of choice. We might even begin with an internet search.

A basic treatment plan will most likely include the management of withdrawal symptoms, therapy, medication for ongoing care, and support groups. With these foundations, individualized treatment has the best chance for bringing about healing, wellness, and long-term sobriety, especially if our substance abuse was triggered by something such as grief.

Is There Healing and Relief Out There?

A lot of times we think of recovery from substance dependence as an all-or-nothing outcome, and this can leave many of us feeling hopeless when considering our chances for recovery. However, as we continue to understand substance dependence as an illness that requires treatment, we can start to see how relapses are a symptom of the illness that must be managed, and treatment involves periodically reassessing and updating our approach as we move forward.

Recovery from substance dependence is a battle, and there needn't be any shame or stigma attached to relapse. Recovery is all about continuing to put one foot in front of the other, one day at a time, taking each moment as it comes and learning coping skills and healthier ways to manage our emotional discomforts.

But recovery *is* possible—with help. Evidence shows that reaching out for help will eventually lead us to finding wellness, recovery, and health again. According to the National Epidemiologic Survey on Alcohol and Related Conditions, "At any given time, of people who could be classified as Dependent in a time prior to the past year, only 25 percent of them are still dependent. That leaves the other 75 percent as no longer Dependent. . . . The odds are that you are three times more likely to end your addiction than you are to continue your addiction!"[3] Hope is there. Therapy as part of treatment can help us learn how to manage our emotional issues as we move forward through our sobriety.

The journey of sobriety and wellness isn't easy. But similar to working toward recovery from other mental health symptoms, we shouldn't feel we have to go it alone. We will find greater success if we surround ourselves with a knowledgeable, supportive, and understanding community that can walk alongside us through the difficult times and into the times of peace, wellness, and good mental health.

What the Bible Says about Substance Abuse

> And do not get drunk on wine, in which lies debauchery, but be filled with the Spirit.
>
> —Ephesians 5:18

The temptation of Jesus as recounted in the Gospel of Matthew 4:1–11 reminds us all that our God willingly allowed himself to experience the entirety of the human condition except sin. He allowed himself to be tempted so that we might feel connected to the infinite, all-powerful Creator of the universe in a deeply intimate way. Rather than believing in a God who stands by simply looking at his creation while we toil under the sufferings of the world he put in motion, we believe in a God who deeply understands our experience as human beings, to the point of not only the miracle of the Incarnation but even the temptations in the desert.

The Bible does not hold back when it comes to the issue of abusing substances: "None who are intoxicated . . . are wise" (Prv 20:1). And yet, while firm in calling out vice and sin in our lives, the Bible always offers a clear and beautiful message of hope: "The God of all grace who called you to his eternal glory through Christ [Jesus] will himself restore, confirm, strengthen, and establish you after you have suffered a little" (1 Pt 5:10–11). After we have walked through darkness, experienced and even fallen victim to temptation, and we feel there's no way we can get our lives back on track, *Christ will restore us*. That's a promise. And God never goes back on his promises.

What the Saints Say about Substance Abuse

> Never be too hard on the man who can't give up drink. It's as hard to give up the drink as it is to raise the dead to life again. But both are possible and even easy for our Lord. We have only to depend on him.
>
> —Venerable Matt Talbot

The message of the Church for those of us suffering with substance dependence is one of clear hope, and one of our beautiful humanity. Perhaps Pope Francis makes that message clearer than anyone else: "Every drug addict has a unique personal story and must be listened to, understood, loved, and, insofar as possible, healed and purified. We cannot stoop to the injustice of categorizing drug addicts as if they were mere objects or broken machines; each person must be valued and appreciated in his or her dignity in order to enable them to be healed. The dignity of the person is what we are called to seek out. They continue to possess, more than ever, a dignity as children of God."[4]

One holy hero who exemplified this message was Venerable Matt Talbot. Born in 1856 in Dublin, Ireland, Matt grew up in a family with a father who was addicted to alcohol, and at just twelve years of age, Matt had to leave school and start working to help support the family. His first job was with a wine merchant, and it was this job that started him on the path toward alcohol dependence.

When working at the docks, his alcoholism only grew worse, to the point where he was out at the pubs every night, running up debts and drinking all of his money away. He even stole a fiddle from a street performer, to sell it for more money to buy alcohol.

When he was twenty-eight years old, he sat outside his favorite pub absolutely broke but hopeful that one of his friends would invite him in for a drink on them. They didn't. He felt he had hit rock bottom, and he immediately went home and told his mother that he would be "taking the pledge," a reference to the practice of abstaining from alcohol for some period of time. Initially he took the pledge for three months, but after finding success with his sobriety, he re-upped his pledge for life and never had another drink.

His sobriety never would have been possible without Matt increasing his devotion to the Catholic faith. He began attending daily Mass, praying, fasting, and serving the poor; he even tried to model his life to that of the sixth-century Irish monks. He practiced mortifications, including wearing a chain around his body to show his devotion to the Blessed Mother and to Jesus through her.

Matt was on his way to Mass on Trinity Sunday in 1925 when he experienced heart failure and died. No one at the scene was able to identify him, but when he was taken to the hospital he was found to have chains all around his body, which eventually led to his sister knowing it was him.

His life is one that shows us there's always hope, even in the darkest moments of addiction, even in the moments where no one else believes that we'll ever find recovery. He's a great intercessor standing by, ready to receive our prayers when we're facing temptation, striving for recovery, or looking for grace to be poured into the hearts of our loved ones.

IN BRIEF

- Substance use disorders are not the fault of the individual suffering or the fault of any loved ones suffering alongside them.
- Addiction is a disease that changes the way the brain functions. Knowing this helps us better understand that people struggling with addiction need treatment and help; just stopping most likely isn't going to be the answer.
- First and foremost, we have to seek out the help of someone who can guide us in getting treatment for our dependence issues.
- A basic treatment plan will most likely include the management of withdrawal symptoms, therapy, medication for ongoing care, and support groups. With these foundations, individualized treatment has the best chance for bringing about healing, wellness, and long-term sobriety.

- The journey of sobriety and wellness isn't easy. We will find greater success if we surround ourselves with a knowledgeable, supportive, and understanding community that can walk alongside us through the difficult times and into the times of peace, wellness, and good mental health.

CLOSING PRAYER

O Most Sweet Jesus, mortify within me all that is bad—make it die. Put to death in me all that is vicious and unruly. Kill whatever displeases Thee, mortify within me all that is my own. Give me true humility, true patience, and true charity.

—Venerable Matt Talbot

CONCLUSION

When I tell people that I'm a marriage and family therapist, I'm inevitably faced with one of three common responses. The most frequent is, "Boy, my family could sure give you plenty to explore and diagnose," followed closely by, "Your wife must feel so blessed to be married to someone who can so openly discuss their feelings." My wife has a hard time holding back her laughter at that one.

The third response when I tell people I'm a therapist and that I work with those walking through a life marked by mental illness: "How do you do it? How do you sit in a room all day and talk with someone like that?"

This response breaks my heart.

Our culture, and yes even our Church, has allowed stigma to creep into our hearts toward those who experience mental illness, seek treatment, or take medication. We even stigmatize talking about the emotional experiences we walk through, which directly leads to many of us avoiding reaching out for help because we see it as a sign of weakness.

Mental illness is *not* the result of a personal failure. We aren't depressed because we did something wrong. We aren't anxious because we don't trust God enough. We aren't grieving because we're weak.

In fact, despite what we might assume, there's almost surely a person sitting in the pews at the same Sunday Mass we're attending who is walking through a similar darkness. They're sitting there, just like us, trying to get through Mass with a smile on their face so no one will know the silent suffering going on in their heart, mind, and soul. They're overwhelmed, just like us, with the idea that they're all alone, that no one on earth could possibly understand what they're going through, let alone even be willing to sit with them to listen or walk alongside them through their suffering.

We live in a world where we pretend that depression, anxiety, symptoms related to trauma, grief and bereavement, and difficulty in relationships aren't something we all experience from time to time, and that's dangerous. It's on us to lead the charge to end it.

The best thing we can do to break the stigma around mental illness in our Church and our communities and to help those suffering from difficult mental and emotional experiences is to talk about it. We have to be willing to share our stories with those we can trust, let people know that they aren't alone, and normalize not only the sharing of our experiences but also the experiences themselves.

We start with being willing to be vulnerable with those we can trust and to share our stories, listen to the stories of others, and create an environment of accompaniment in our Church, our communities, and our homes. We start by helping people see that they aren't alone, they aren't failures, and God hasn't abandoned them. We remember not to overspiritualize mental illness, but at the same time remember that God is a loving and personal God who wants to bring good out of every single experience we have, no matter how dark. We equip our priests, religious sisters, parish staff, and ministry leaders with the tools to identify mental health symptoms and assist our sisters and brothers in need with knowing what steps they can take to get help. We create a community in our parish that brings meals to those who are suffering, helps people who are unable to get to Mass still feel connected to the faith, and welcomes everyone, no matter how they might be feeling mentally and emotionally.

We have to learn to feel comfortable saying, "Yes, I understand. I've also felt abandoned, hopeless, like God doesn't care, and like I couldn't even bring myself to pray," and then share how things shifted, how God revealed himself, and how hope and healing came to us in order to give hope and healing to another. We have to learn to feel comfortable saying, "I've been there. I've felt like I wanted to die. I prayed for God to take my life because I didn't want to go on," and then share how a light showed up in the darkness and helped us keep putting one foot in front of the other. We have to feel comfortable sharing that even though we've gone through difficulties and then found healing, we still slip back into our struggles from time to time and that it's okay.

And we have to learn to be okay with saying, "I'm not doing well right now." It's okay to not be okay, to not be filled with Christian joy at every moment of our lives. Life is often one trial after the next. We strive to grow closer to God, only to be faced with the death of a loved one, the loss of a job, the breakup of a family, or a traumatic event we wouldn't wish on anyone.

But somehow, through all of it, God is there, silently suffering alongside us. When we can't see him, when we feel all alone, that's when we most desperately need a community of people who are willing to sit with us and walk with us and not be scared by our thoughts and emotions. And when we can, we need to be that for someone else who is suffering.

Remember, we are not less than because we experience mental illness or mental health symptoms of any kind. We are not less loved, less lovable, less children of God, less capable—less anything. Instead, we offer the Church something it so dearly needs in order to help the suffering of this world. We have experience, the understanding of the Cross, and hope, and we can give all of that to those who are desperately asking for it for our Church.

After all, *we are the Church*. We are the ones who will lead the Church into a healthier understanding of how to help those with mental illness as Christ would want his Church to lead.

May the words of St. Óscar Romero be our reminder and our inspiration as we go forward on this mission: "There are some things that can only be seen through eyes that have cried." Through our own eyes that have cried, may we see the face of Christ in every suffering sister and brother we meet, and respond exactly as he would want us to respond.

ACKNOWLEDGMENTS

This book wouldn't exist without an aging high school AP psychology teacher inspiring me way back in 1999. Even though I was years from having to make any big life decisions, her class set me on the path that got me where I am today. The stories she would teach us from social psychology and early psychological theories prompted me to delve further into the field and to absolutely fall in love with it. With many more inspiring professors in undergrad and graduate worlds, I continued to enjoy learning all about the reasons why we are the way we are and do the things we do.

After my first traineeship in the field, I realized something else that would shape the course of my journey as a therapist: I *really* didn't have a passion for doing weekly therapy with the working well. Not that they didn't need the help, but the work simply didn't click with me. I left that traineeship and got a new one at a residential program for those living with chronic and severe mental illness, and it absolutely changed my life. I was immediately drawn to working with those suffering from schizophrenia, bipolar disorder, major depression, PTSD, OCD, eating disorders, various personality disorders, and the like, and it was that second traineeship that defined the rest of my career.

I was blessed beyond measure to get an opportunity to be a case manager and therapist in community mental health back in 2005, and I have been working in that field ever since. Working in that field, one can't help but become an advocate for this population, an advocate for wanting to dismantle the stigma that weighs so heavily on them and everyone who walks alongside them.

I am grateful to the incredible team at Ave Maria Press for being open to working with me on this book. It isn't easy to say yes to a book about the intersection of mental health and the Catholic faith, but the Ave team has been nothing but excited, engaged, and helpful with joining the battle to end stigma in our world, our communities, and our Church.

I would also like to thank every person who has ever listened to, shared, or sent in questions to the *St. Dymphna's Playbook* podcast, and to Fr. Anthony Sciarappa and Fr. Harrison Ayre for inviting me—me, a lowly layperson—on *their* podcast to discuss mental health, which got me started down this path in the first place.

Of course, if it weren't for my family, *none of this* could have ever happened. My wife, Karen, is the partner God brought into my life without me deserving her in the least, and I pray every day that I can return her to him through the graces of our marriage. My children—James, Paul, Andrew, Luke, and Charlie—have not only been the joy of my life on a daily basis but also literally saved me from depression, grief, and heartbreak. They have shown me the love of Christ and consistently provide me with opportunities to grow into the person God wants me to be.

Last, but not least, I have to give my love to St. Dymphna herself. A patron of my work and close friend throughout my life, I long for the day I get to meet her in heaven and give her a big hug—she's going to have to pray *a lot* to help me get there.

RESOURCES

National Suicide Prevention Lifeline: 1-800-273-8255

Crisis Text Line: Text HOME to 741741

National Domestic Violence Hotline: 1-800-799-SAFE (7233)

SAMHSA National Substance Abuse Helpline: 1-800-662-4357

Veteran's Crisis Line: 1-800-273-8255

National Alliance on Mental Illness (for family members): https://www.nami.org

For veterans: https://www.mentalhealth.va.gov

For older adults: https://www.ncoa.org/center-for-healthy-aging/behavioral-health

For college students: https://www.jedfoundation.org

For the LGBTQ population: https://www.thetrevorproject.org

For anxiety and depression: https://adaa.org

For depression and bipolar support: https://www.dbsalliance.org

For schizophrenia and related disorders: https://sardaa.org

For eating disorders: https://www.nationaleatingdisorders.org

For domestic violence: https://www.safehorizon.org

For grief and bereavement:
https://www.counseling.org/knowledge-center/mental-health-resources/grief-and-loss-resources

NOTES

Introduction: Lord, the One You Love Is Sick

1. "The Final Word Is Love," *Catholic Worker*, May 1980, https://www.catholicworker.org/dorothyday/articles/867.html.

2. Anne Thériault, "Geel, Belgium Has a Radical Approach to Mental Illness," *Broadview*, September 5, 2019, https://broadview.org/geel-belgium-mental-health.

3. Thériault, "Geel, Belgium Has a Radical Approach to Mental Illness."

1. Anhedonia: Lord, the One You Love Feels Nothing

1. For a complete listing of symptoms of major depressive disorder and additional notes on the diagnosis, see American Psychiatric Association, *Diagnostic and Statistical Manual of Mental Disorders*, 5th ed. (Washington, DC: American Psychiatric Association, 2013).

2. Margarita Tartakovsky, "When You Don't Feel Anything during Your Depression," Psych Central, April 9, 2018, https://psychcentral.com/blog/when-you-dont-feel-anything-during-your-depression.

3. "Six Holistic Ways to Treat Anhedonia," Tree House Recovery, accessed May 6, 2021, https://treehouserecovery.com/treating-anhedonia.

4. James Martin, "Don't Call Me a Saint?" *America*, November 14, 2012, https://www.americamagazine.org/content/all-things/dont-call-me-saint.

5. Mother Teresa, Wikipedia, last modified April 10, 2021, https://en.wikipedia.org/wiki/Mother_Teresa.

6. Joan Graff Clucas, *Mother Teresa* (New York: Chelsea House Publications, 1988), 35.

7. David Scott, "Mother Teresa's Long Dark Night," Catholic Education Resource Center, accessed May 6, 2021, https://www.catholiceducation.org/en/faith-and-character/faith-and-character/mother-teresas-long-dark-night.html.

2. Irritability: Lord, the One You Love Is Annoyed with Everything

1. Mohammad Ali Besharat, Mahin Eternadi Nia, and Hojatollah Farahani, "Anger and Major Depressive Disorder: The Mediating Role of Emotion Regulation and Anger Rumination," *Asian Journal of Psychiatry* 6, no. 1 (February 2013): 35–41, doi:10.1016/j.ajp.2012.07.013.

2. "Recognizing and Addressing Depression Presenting as Anger," Online MSW Programs, April 2020, https://www.onlinemswprograms.com/resources/social-issues/addressing-depression-presenting-as-anger.

3. Meg Hunter-Kilmer, "What We Probably Don't Know about St. Jerome Is Just What We Need to Know," Aleteia, September 28, 2017, https://aleteia.org/2017/09/28/what-we-probably-dont-know-about-st-jerome-is-just-what-we-need-to-know.

4. "St. James, Spain and Anger Management," iBenedictines, July 25, 2012, https://www.ibenedictines.org/2012/07/25/st-james-spain-and-anger-management.

5. Nancy L. Roberts, *Dorothy Day and the Catholic Worker* (New York: SUNY Press, 1985), 95.

6. José María Román, "St. Vincent de Paul, a Biography—the Story of His Captivity," We Are Vincentians, December 24, 2016, http://vincentians.com/en/saint-vincent-paul-biography-04-the-story-of-his-captivity.

7. Omar F. A. Gutiérrez, "The Irritable Saint and the King of Love: St. Vincent de Paul," We Are Vincentians, January 14, 2016, http://vincentians.com/en/the-irritable-saint-and-the-king-of-love-st-vincent-de-paul.

8. “St. Vincent de Paul,” Saint of the Day, Franciscan Media, September 27, 2020, https://www.franciscanmedia.org/saint-vincent-de-paul.

3. Fatigue: Lord, the One You Love Is Tired

1. Helia Ghanean, Amanda K. Ceniti, and Sidney H. Kennedy, “Fatigue in Patients with Major Depressive Disorder: Prevalence, Burden and Pharmacological Approaches to Management,” *CNS Drugs* 32 (2018): 65–74, https://doi.org/10.1007/s40263-018-0490-z.

2. Paige Smith, “Why Depression Makes You So Damn Tired All the Time,” *HuffPost*, February 20, 2019, https://www.huffpost.com/entry/depression-tired_l_5c6c3fcae4b012225acd8663.

3. “5 Tips for Dealing with the Overwhelming Fatigue of Depression,” Psych Central, April 17, 2015, https://psychcentral.com/blog/5-tips-for-dealing-with-the-overwhelming-fatigue-of-depression.

4. “5 Tips for Dealing with the Overwhelming Fatigue of Depression.”

5. “5 Tips for Dealing with the Overwhelming Fatigue of Depression.”

6. “Mary Magdalene de’ Pazzi,” Wikipedia, last modified February 16, 2021, https://en.wikipedia.org/wiki/Mary_Magdalene_de%27_Pazzi.

7. Paolo O. Pirlo, “St. Mary Magdalene de Pazzi,” *My First Book of Saints* (Paranaque City: Sons of Holy Mary Immaculate–Quality Catholic Publications, 1997), 106–7.

8. “Saint Mary Magdalene de Pazzi,” *Thy Sins Are Forgiven* (blog), May 25, 2105, http://thysinsareforgiven.com/?p=2216.

4. Hopelessness: Lord, the One You Love Doesn’t Want to Go On

1. This practice is suggested by Bill Knaus in “Overcome Hopelessness Thinking and Stop Feeling Depressed,” *Psychology Today*, February 28, 2015, https://www.psychologytoday.com/us/blog/

science-and-sensibility/201502/overcome-hopelessness-thinking-and-stop-feeling-depressed.

2. John M. Grohol, "15 Common Cognitive Distortions," Psych Central, May 17, 2016, https://psychcentral.com/lib/15-common-cognitive-distortions.

3. John M. Grohol, "10 Proven Methods for Fixing Cognitive Distortions," Psych Central, May 17, 2016, https://psychcentral.com/lib/fixing-cognitive-distortions.

4. Therese J. Borchard, "9 Types of Hopelessness and How to Overcome Them," Psych Central, October 14, 2009, https://psychcentral.com/blog/the-9-types-of-hopelessness-and-how-to-overcome-them.

5. Anna Rose Meeds, "Suffering from Mental Illness with the Saints," Catholic Stand, March 12, 2014, https://www.catholicstand.com/suffering-saints-mental-illness.

6. "Clara (1697–1744)," Encyclopedia.com, accessed May 7, 2021, https://www.encyclopedia.com/women/encyclopedias-almanacs-transcripts-and-maps/clara-1697-1744.

7. Meeds, "Suffering from Mental Illness with the Saints," https://www.catholicstand.com/suffering-saints-mental-illness.

6. Social Anxiety: Lord, the One You Love Is Self-Conscious

1. "Social Anxiety Disorder: More Than Just Shyness," National Institute of Mental Health, accessed May 6, 2021, https://www.nimh.nih.gov/health/publications/social-anxiety-disorder-more-than-just-shyness/index.shtml.

2. Barbara Markway, "Must-Have Coping Strategies for Social Anxiety," *Psychology Today*, May 14, 2013, https://www.psychologytoday.com/us/blog/shyness-is-nice/201305/must-have-coping-strategies-social-anxiety.

3. Markway, "Must-Have Coping Strategies for Social Anxiety."

4. "Treating Social Anxiety Disorder," *Harvard Health*, March 2010, https://www.health.harvard.edu/newsletter_article/treating-social-anxiety-disorder.

5. "Treating Social Anxiety Disorder."

6. Vincent J. O'Malley, *Ordinary Suffering of Extraordinary Saints* (Huntington, IN: Our Sunday Visitor, 1999), 38.

7. "Thérèse of Lisieux," Wikipedia, last modified April 15, 2021, https://en.wikipedia.org/wiki/Thérèse_of_Lisieux#cite_note-15.

8. "Thérèse of Lisieux."

7. Obsessive-Compulsive Disorder: Lord, the One You Love Is Battling Intrusive Thoughts

1. "What Is Obsessive-Compulsive Disorder?" American Psychiatric Association, accessed May 6, 2021, https://www.psychiatry.org/patients-families/ocd/what-is-obsessive-compulsive-disorder.

2. "What Is OCD?" International OCD Foundation, accessed May 6, 2021, https://iocdf.org/about-ocd.

3. "What Is OCD?"

4. "Treatments for OCD," Anxiety and Depression Association of America, accessed May 6, 2021, https://adaa.org/understanding-anxiety/obsessive-compulsive-disorder-ocd/treatments-for-ocd.

5. Kamryn T. Eddy, Lissa Dutra, Rebekah Bradley, and Drew Westen, "A Multidimensional Meta-Analysis of Psychotherapy and Pharmacotherapy for Obsessive-Compulsive Disorder," *Clinical Psychology Review* 24, no. 8 (2004): 1011–30, doi:10.1016/j.cpr.2004.08.004.

6. A couple workbooks I have found helpful are Bruce Hyman, *The OCD Workbook: Your Guide to Breaking Free from Obsessive-Compulsive Disorder* (Oakland, CA: New Harbinger Publications, 2010); and Jon Hershfield and Tom Corboy, *The Mindfulness Workbook for OCD: A Guide to Overcoming Obsessions and Compulsions Using Mindfulness and Cognitive Behavioral Therapy* (Oakland, CA: New Harbinger Publications, 2013).

7. Michael A. Hayes and David Tombs, *Truth and Memory: The Church and Human Rights in El Salvador and Guatemala* (Leominster, UK: Gracewing, 2001).

8. Peter Jesserer Smith, "Miracle Spotlights the Real Oscar Romero: A Daily Path of Holiness Made a Martyr," *National*

Catholic Register, April 13, 2017, https://www.ncregister.com/daily-news/miracle-spotlights-the-real-oscar-romero-a-daily-path-of-holiness-made-a-ma.

8. Scrupulosity: Lord, the One You Love Has Religious OCD

1. International OCD Foundation, "Scrupulosity" (Boston: International OCD Foundation, 2010), https://iocdf.org/wp-content/uploads/2014/10/IOCDF-Scrupulosity-Fact-Sheet.pdf.

2. International OCD Foundation, "Scrupulosity."

3. International OCD Foundation, "Scrupulosity."

4. Ted Witzig Jr., "Coping Statements for Christians with OCD and Scrupulosity," ACCFS, May 12, 2020, https://www.accounseling.org/coping-statements-for-christians-with-ocd-scrupulosity.

5. International OCD Foundation, "Scrupulosity."

6. Examples drawn from "Living with Religious OCD," Made of Millions, accessed March 10, 2021, https://www.madeofmillions.com/ocd/religious-ocd.

7. Kevin Foss, "Scrupulosity OCD Treatment Shouldn't Be a Hard Sell," *Psychology Today*, November 26, 2019, https://www.psychologytoday.com/us/blog/stronger-fear/201911/scrupulosity-ocd-treatment-shouldnt-be-hard-sell.

8. "Satanist to Saint," Catholic Bible 101, accessed May 6, 2021, https://www.catholicbible101.com/satanisttosaint.htm.

9. "Bartolo Longo," Wikipedia, last modified November 5, 2020, https://en.wikipedia.org/wiki/Bartolo_Longo.

9. Post-Traumatic Stress Disorder: Lord, the One You Love Feels Helpless

1. Natalie Boyd, "Learned Helplessness: Seligman's Theory and Depression," Study.com, last updated June 19, 2020, https://study.com/academy/lesson/how-seligmans-learned-helplessness-theory-applies-to-human-depression-and-stress.html.

2. "PTSD Fact Sheet: Frequently Asked Questions," Brainline, November 28, 2017, https://www.brainline.org/article/ptsd-fact-sheet-frequently-asked-questions.

3. "Post-Traumatic Stress Disorder," National Institute of Mental Health, last modified May 2019, https://www.nimh.nih.gov/health/topics/post-traumatic-stress-disorder-ptsd/index.shtml.

4. Lawrence Robinson, Melinda Smith, and Jeanne Segal, "Emotional and Psychological Trauma," HelpGuide, last updated February 2020, https://www.helpguide.org/articles/ptsd-trauma/coping-with-emotional-and-psychological-trauma.htm.

5. Wyatt Myers, "Post-Traumatic Stress Disorder Prognosis," Everyday Health, January 17, 2011, https://www.everydayhealth.com/anxiety/post-traumatic-stress-disorder-prognosis.aspx.

6. "What Is EMDR?" EMDR Institute, accessed March 11, 2021, https://www.emdr.com/what-is-emdr.

7. James D. Herbert, Scott O. Lilienfeld, Jeffrey M. Lohr, Robert W. Montgomery, William T. O'Donohue, Gerald M. Rosen, and David F. Tolin, "Science and Pseudoscience in the Development of Eye Movement Desensitization and Reprocessing: Implications for Clinical Psychology," *Clinical Psychology Review* 20, no. 8 (November 2000): 945–71.

8. Herbert et al., "Science and Pseudoscience in the Development of Eye Movement Desensitization and Reprocessing," 945–71.

9. Fulton J. Sheen, *The Moral Universe* (London: Aeterna Press, 2015), 4.

10. "Blessed Laura Vicuña (1891–1904)," Salesians of Don Bosco, UK. Archived 2007-06-09 at the Wayback Machine.

10. Dissociation: Lord, the One You Love Is Feeling Detached

1. Matthew Tull, "What Is Dissociation?" Verywell Mind, July 19, 2020, https://www.verywellmind.com/dissociation-2797292.

2. Modified from Arielle Schwartz, "Complex PTSD and Dissociation," April 26, 2016, https://drarielleschwartz.com/complex-ptsd-and-dissociation-dr-arielle-schwartz.

3. "Dissociative Disorders," Mayo Clinic, November 17, 2017, https://www.mayoclinic.org/diseases-conditions/dissociative-disorders/diagnosis-treatment/drc-20355221.

4. Corinne G. Dempsey, "Lessons in Miracles from Kerala, South India: Stories of Three 'Christian' Saints," *History of Religions* 39, no. 2 (1999): 150–76.

5. "Alphonsa of the Immaculate Conception (1910–1946)," Vatican.va, https://www.vatican.va/news_services/liturgy/saints/2008/ns_lit_doc_20081012_alfonsa_en.html.

11. Self-Destructiveness: Lord, the One You Love Is Hurting Themselves

1. "Self-Harm," National Alliance on Mental Illness, accessed May 7, 2021, https://www.nami.org/About-Mental-Illness/Common-with-Mental-Illness/Self-harm.

2. Raychelle Cassada Lohmann, "Understanding Suicide and Self-Harm: Discovering the Similarities and Differences between Self-Harm and Suicide," *Psychology Today*, October 28, 2012, https://www.psychologytoday.com/us/blog/teen-angst/201210/understanding-suicide-and-self-harm.

3. "Self-Injury (Cutting, Self-Harm, or Self-Mutilation)," Mental Health America, accessed May 7, 2021, https://www.mhanational.org/conditions/self-injury-cutting-self-harm-or-self-mutilation.

4. Erika Kilburn and Janis Whitlock, *Distraction Techniques and Alternative Coping Strategies*, Practical Matters Series, Cornell Research Program on Self-Injury and Recovery (Ithaca, NY: Cornell University, 2009).

5. Mayo Clinic Staff, "Self-Injury/Cutting," Mayo Clinic, December 7, 2018, https://www.mayoclinic.org/diseases-conditions/self-injury/diagnosis-treatment/drc-20350956.

6. Catherine of Siena, *Letters of Catherine Benincasa* (self-pub., CreateSpace Independent Publishing Platform, 2015).

7. "Rose of Lima," Wikipedia, last modified April 26, 2021, https://en.wikipedia.org/wiki/Rose_of_Lima.

8. "St. Rose of Lima," Dominican Sisters of Saint Cecilia, accessed May 7, 2021, https://www.nashvilledominican.org/community/our-dominican-heritage/our-saints-and-blesseds/st-rose-lima.

12. Loneliness: Lord, the One You Love Is Isolated

1. Cigna, *Cigna 2018 U.S. Loneliness Index* (Bloomfield, CT: Cigna Health Corporation, 2018), https://www.cigna.com/assets/docs/newsroom/loneliness-survey-2018-updated-fact-sheet.pdf.

2. US Department of Veterans Affairs, *Loneliness—a Risk Factor for Suicide* (Washington, DC: US Department of Veterans Affairs, 2020), https://www.mentalhealth.va.gov/suicide_prevention/docs/Literature-Review-Loneliness-CLEARED-3-5-19.pdf.

3. California Institute of Technology, "How Social Isolation Transforms the Brain: A Particular Neural Chemical Is Overproduced during Long-Term Social Isolation, Causing Increased Aggression and Fear," *ScienceDaily*, May 17, 2018, www.sciencedaily.com/releases/2018/05/180517113856.htm.

4. "Social Withdrawal/Isolation," Make the Connection, accessed May 7, 2021, https://maketheconnection.net/symptoms/social-withdrawal.

5. Edward Lecompte, *Glory of the Mohawks: The Life of the Venerable Catherine Tekakwitha*, trans. Florence Ralston Werum (Milwaukee: Bruce Publishing, 1944), 28; Francis X. Weiser, *Kateri Tekakwitha* (Caughnawaga, Canada: Kateri Center, 1972), 65–68.

6. K. I. Koppedrayer, "The Making of the First Iroquois Virgin: Early Jesuit Biographies of the Blessed Kateri Tekakwitha," *Ethnohistory* 40, no. 2 (1993): 277–306.

13. Resentment: Lord, the One You Love Is Keeping Score

1. Dianne Grande, "Couple's Therapy: Does It Really Work?" *Psychology Today*, December 6, 2017, https://www.psychologytoday.

com/us/blog/in-it-together/201712/couples-therapy-does-it-really-work.

2. "St. Rita of Cascia," *Catholic News Agency*, accessed May 7, 2021, https://www.catholicnewsagency.com/saint/st-rita-of-cascia-464.

14. Feeling Stagnant: Lord, the One You Love Is Going Nowhere . . . Fast

1. Glenn Dellaire, "Victim Souls Are Co-Redeemers with Christ," St. Gemma Galgani, accessed May 7, 2021, https://www.stgemmagalgani.com/2009/07/co-redeemers-with-christ-victim-souls.html.

15. Manipulative Relationships: Lord, the One You Love Is Being Exploited

1. Preston Ni, "How to Recognize and Handle Manipulative Relationships," *Psychology Today*, July 13, 2014, https://www.psychologytoday.com/us/blog/communication-success/201407/how-recognize-and-handle-manipulative-relationships.

2. Cassie Shortsleeve, "How to Tell If Someone Is Manipulating You—and What to Do about It," *Time*, October 16, 2018, https://time.com/5411624/how-to-tell-if-being-manipulated.

3. Ni, "How to Recognize and Handle Manipulative Relationships."

4. Sheri Stritof, "How to Recognize and React to Manipulation in Your Marriage," Verywell Mind, February 5, 2020, https://www.verywellmind.com/manipulation-in-marriage-2302245.

5. Ni, "How to Recognize and Handle Manipulative Relationships."

16. Abusive Relationships: Lord, the One You Love Is Being Harmed

1. REACH Team, "6 Different Types of Abuse," REACH Beyond Domestic Violence, March 23, 2017, https://reachma.org/6-different-types-abuse.
2. REACH Team, "6 Different Types of Abuse."
3. REACH Team, "6 Different Types of Abuse."
4. REACH Team, "6 Different Types of Abuse."
5. Sherri Gordon, "What Is Emotional Abuse?" Verywell Mind, September 17, 2020, https://www.verywellmind.com/identify-and-cope-with-emotional-abuse-4156673.
6. Gordon, "What Is Emotional Abuse?"
7. "Should I Go to Couples Therapy with My Abusive Partner?" National Domestic Violence Hotline, accessed May 7, 2021, https://www.thehotline.org/2014/08/01/why-we-dont-recommend-couples-counseling-for-abusive-relationships.
8. Sharie Stines, "Why Couples Counseling Doesn't Work in Abusive Relationships," Psych Central, August 27, 2015, https://pro.psychcentral.com/why-couples-counseling-doesnt-work-in-abusive-relationships.
9. "National Marriage Week: An Example of Faithful Love, Enduring Unto Death (Bl. Elizabeth Canori Mora)," *Marriage: Unique for a Reason*, February 9, 2012, http://www.marriageuniqueforareason.org/2012/02/09/national-marriage-week-an-example-of-faithful-love-enduring-unto-death-bl-elizabeth-canori-mora.
10. "National Marriage Week."

17. Heartbreak: Lord, the One You Love Is Crushed by Grief

1. Deborah Khoshaba, "About Complicated Bereavement Disorder," *Psychology Today*, September 28, 2013, https://www.psychologytoday.com/us/blog/get-hardy/201309/about-complicated-bereavement-disorder-0.

2. For a more complete list of symptoms, see Khoshaba, "About Complicated Bereavement Disorder."

3. "Coping with Grief and Loss," HelpGuide, September 2020, https://www.helpguide.org/articles/grief/coping-with-grief-and-loss.htm.

4. Steps modified from Nina Radcliff, "How to Deal with Death, Loss, Grief, and Bereavement," *Washington Times*, May 1, 2017, https://www.washingtontimes.com/news/2017/may/1/health-how-deal-death-loss-grief-bereavement.

5. Chloe Langr, "3 Women Saints Who Know the Pain of Miscarriage," *Aleteia*, August 20, 2018, https://aleteia.org/2018/08/20/3-women-saints-who-know-the-pain-of-miscarriage/2.

18. Joylessness: Lord, the One You Love Doesn't Even Want to Feel Better

1. "Mourning and Memory: A Paradoxical Grief," Association for Psychological Science, January 11, 2013, https://www.psychologicalscience.org/news/were-only-human/mourning-and-memory-a-paradoxical-grief.html.

2. Katherine C. Nordal, "Grief: Coping with the Loss of Your Loved One," American Psychological Association, January 1, 2020, https://www.apa.org/topics/grief.

3. "Complicated Grief," Mayo Clinic, accessed May 7, 2021, https://www.mayoclinic.org/diseases-conditions/complicated-grief/diagnosis-treatment/drc-20360389.

4. Kim Glickman, quoted in Bruce Jancin, "Complicated Grief Treatment Gets Better Results than Interpersonal Psychotherapy," *Clinical Psychiatry News*, May 26, 2017, https://www.mdedge.com/psychiatry/article/139212/depression/complicated-grief-treatment-gets-better-results-interpersonal.

5. Simone Troisi and Cristiana Paccini, *Chiara Corbella Petrillo: A Witness to Joy* (Bedford, NH: Sophia Institute Press, 2015).

6. "The Life of Saint Elizabeth Ann Seton," Seton Shrine, accessed May 7, 2021, https://setonshrine.org/elizabeth-ann-seton.

19. Powerlessness: Lord, the One You Love Feels Weak

1. Mary Zemites, "Grief and Powerlessness," Webhealing.com, May 23, 2013, https://webhealing.com/grief-and-powerlessness.

2. Stephanie O'Neill, "Coronavirus Has Upended Our World. It's OK to Grieve," NPR, March 26, 2020, https://www.npr.org/sections/health-shots/2020/03/26/820304899/coronavirus-has-upended-our-world-its-ok-to-grieve.

3. Troisi and Paccini, *Chiara Corbella Petrillo*.

20. Substance Abuse: Lord, the One You Love Is Self-Medicating

1. National Institute on Drug Addiction, quoted in "The Science of Addiction," Shatterproof, accessed March 22, 2021, https://www.shatterproof.org/about-addiction/science-of-addiction.

2. "Science of Addiction."

3. Steven Slate, "Substance Dependence Recovery Rates: With and Without Treatment," Clean Slate Addiction Site, accessed March 22, 2021, http://www.thecleanslate.org/self-change/substance-dependence-recovery-rates-with-and-without-treatment.

4. Francis, "Address of His Holiness Pope Francis to Participants in the Meeting Sponsored by the Pontifical Academy of Sciences on 'Narcotics: Problems and Solutions to This Global Issue,'" Libreria Editrice Vaticana, November 24, 2016, https://www.vatican.va/content/francesco/en/speeches/2016/november/documents/papa-francesco_20161124_seminario-accademia-scienze.html.

Tommy Tighe is a marriage and family therapist, creator of the *Saint Dymphna's Playbook* podcast, and the cohost of *Repent and Submit* on CatholicTV. He is the author of *The Catholic Hipster Handbook*, *The Catholic Hipster: The Next Level*, and *#BlessedMother*. He is the coauthor of *How To: Catholic Family* and *Catholic Funny Fill-Ins* with his wife Karen.

Tighe has appeared on Relevant Radio, EWTN Radio, and The Catholic Channel on SiriusXM Radio—the station that runs his podcast *The Chimney*. He has contributed to publications that include *Angelus News*, *Catholic Herald*, *CatholicMom.com*, *Aleteia*, and *Catholic Digest*.

He lives with his family in the San Francisco Bay Area of California.

catholichipster.com
Twitter: @theghissilent
Instagram: catholichipster

ALSO BY **TOMMY TIGHE**

The Catholic Hipster Handbook

Rediscovering Cool Saints, Forgotten Prayers, and Other Weird but Sacred Stuff

Being a Catholic Hipster is all about an attitude—an attitude grounded in being part of a nonmainstream community of believers dedicated to something bigger than themselves in a world dominated by self-centeredness. It's about yearning to learn more about the faith by seeking out "Catholic cool"—overlooked saints, forgotten prayers and feast days, and traditional practices long set aside by mainstream believers. In *The Catholic Hipster Handbook*, Tommy Tighe explores the beautiful weirdness of the Catholic Church to help you grow in your faith in unconventional ways.

"Mysticism, joy, and general weirdness."

—From the foreword by **Jeannie Gaffigan**

Comedienne, actress, and writer

Catholic Hipster: The Next Level

How Some Awesomely Obscure Stuff Helps Us Live Our Faith with Passion

Building on the overwhelming popularity of *The Catholic Hipster Handbook*, Tommy Tighe presents a new cast of fellow hipsters in this follow up book—including Haley Stewart, Samantha Povlock, Matthew Sewell, Fr. Damian Ferrence, and Patrick Neve—to share overlooked saints, forgotten prayers, and profound practices that define the nonmainstream Catholic lifestyle, inspiring you to live your faith in dynamic ways.

"This book has something for everyone."

Sr. Theresa Aletheia Noble, F.S.P.